Today is the Day!

Healthy Junk is published and distributed by True Living Health Products, an entity dedicated to creating and providing products true to health. If you are interested in seeing other healthful products that we offer please visit our website at: www.truelivinghealthproducts.com

Also:
Feel free to e-mail questions, comments or suggestions to:
truelivinghealthproducts@gmail.com

Copyright © 2014 by True Living Health Products. All rights reserved. No part of this publication may be reproduced, distributed, or transmitted in any form or by any means, including photocopying, recording, or other electronic or mechanical methods without the prior written permission of the publisher, except in the case of brief quotations embodied in critical reviews and certain other noncommercial uses permitted by copyright law. For permission requests send e-mail to truelivinghealthproducts@gmail.com

Contents

Preface iv
About the Authors v
Introduction vi

Chapter 1 — Raw vs. Cooked 1

Chapter 2 — Anti-Nutrition 5
   Our Dear Friend—The Body 7

Chapter 3 — PH Connection 9

Chapter 4 — The Power of Green 13
   Go With The Flow 17

Chapter 5 — Sprouting 19
   Sprouting Guide 21

Chapter 6 — Fermenting 33

Chapter 7 — Vices Made Nicer 37

Chapter 8 — Tips & Tidbits 43
   The Big Picture 49

Chapter 9 — Food Preparation 51
   Kitchen Essentials 51
   Chef Basics 54
   Foods to Have on Hand 55

Chapter 10 — Recipes 57
   Recipe Key 58
   Recipe Index 59
   Beverages & Bliss Blends 63
   Breakfast Foods 75
   Snacks 83
   Salads & Dressings 91
   Soups 101
   Main Meals 109
   Sauces/Spreads/Dips 129
   Condiments 143
   Desserts & Better Baked Goods 147

Ingredient Definitions 166

Resources 169

Preface

Healthy Junk?...

Yes! Every body can be happy! We can make cake and eat it too!

Foods are not inherently "bad", their ill fate is the deed of processing, refinement, growing practices, improper preparation methods, additives, etc. *Of course the reason these foods are bad for us is because we consume them...and the reason they're available is because we do!*

We have a choice!

The focus of Healthy Junk is not only on minimizing the bad, but on maximizing the presence of good as well—elevating foods potential to provide more nutrition, more taste, and more satisfaction. You will find a sensible approach to health and nourishment as well as economy and convenience that naturally supports sustainability and kindness to the earth and its inhabitants.

Our recipes include many of the foods you have come to love...and now they are here to love you back! Consider a truce between the healthfully conscious angel and the purely pleasure seeking devil—a balance between nutrition and satisfaction.

Healthy Junk utilizes the highly beneficial practices of sprouting, fermenting, and proper cooking methods to allow for endless healthful possibilities. Along with its recipes, Healthy Junk provides insight and information to generate and benefit life while eliminating the need for constant restraint from it.

Enjoy!

About the Authors

Hello! We are Mark & Kim Johnson. It is in the foothills of the Sierra Nevada Mountains of Northern California in the midst of over 100 fruiting trees, bushes, vines, and gardens that we operate a small business we call True Living Health Products. Our passion for living has led us to the creating and offering of various health and fitness products, the nourishing of crowds at special events, and the teaching of an assortment of classes that focus on the true aspects of living well.

Kim has been involved in the field of natural health and healing for over 20 years with formal training in Nutrition, Ayurveda, and Herbalism, with focus on the relationship between body and mind.

Marks pursuit in health and fitness occurred at a very young age and has led to national certification as a personal trainer, the inventing and creating of various types of fitness equipment, and the authoring of several health related books.

Together our journey has led to the un-processing of the fads, the miracles, and the fanatic to reveal vitality and health through a simpler and gentler way of living. Our true attainment has come through the inspiration and gratitude we experience for all life and the true sense of being that cannot be achieved solely through the body. We are all inherently born into this gift and only need to recognize its presence to nourish and heal every facet of our existence.

And so it is in gratitude that we care for the body and the occupation of the mind, for they are the vehicles that carry our experience of life!

In gratitude, Mark and Kim

Introduction

Welcome to *Healthy Junk,* where intention and attention are on *pro-creating—that is* to increase benefit to life through proper sourcing, preparation, and consumption congruent to all life.

The tide of convenience and cheap food is wearing away the very shores that we call health and home. A wiser and healthier way of living lies within the natural flow of life–remaining sustainable and beneficial to all throughout time. It begins with replacing refined, packaged, and processed foods from far away, with seasonally fresh locally grown whole foods produced in an earth friendly environment that provide the proper food and nutrition we were designed for.

The methods of sprouting, fermenting, and proper cooking are also procreating practices which offer greater benefits to our well being. The life giving process of sprouting seeds, nuts, grains, and legumes generate nutrients that in turn are more life giving, vital, and usable in our bodies while simultaneously diminishing and eliminating non-nutrients and other naturally occurring toxins.

Fermentation is a pro-life process utilized throughout the ages and still by many today. For their ability to break down harmful substances, increase nutrition, preserve and cure, these foods provide benefits that can not be over-rated. *These foods play an important role in our life, as our entire inner ecosystem requires and benefits from the procreative micro organisms they provide. Their protection and prevention from harmful bacteria, virus and disease are of invaluable consequence.*

Proper cooking techniques further increase the edibility and value of certain foods that may otherwise be useless or even harmful without them. *Cooking provides the ability and option to widen our diet/nutritional intake through variety.*

We have found that through utilizing the beneficial methods of sprouting, fermenting, and proper cooking, a higher and more valuable content of nutrients are introduced and assimilated. This becomes evident through the gain and balance of physical and mental health, satiation, and freedom from cravings.

There is much to be aware of concerning the health, safety, treatment, and future of our food supply. Throughout this book we work at fostering ways of obtaining, creating, and consuming foods true to health and true to humanity. *While this excludes the use of animal products, the judgment is not in their use but within the methods, treatments, and consequences of producing such food.*

Chapter 1

Raw vs. Cooked

We know...your thinking Good vs. Evil—a fight to see who wins... but this isn't about fighting, it's about winning! The following are strategies that reward us with the most beneficial elements available within our food.

Although it is true that fresh whole raw foods generally contain more vitamins, enzymes, and other nutrients than their cooked counterparts, there is more to it than meets the fork. It's not only in heating that we see losses in nutrients, exposure to water, air, light, improper storage and age all have their impact on the vitality of our food. *How food is prepared can dramatically change its nutrient content.*

Many foods in their natural state contain varying forms and amounts of toxins and/or anti-nutrients that Mother Nature provided for the purpose of self preservation. These foods become more beneficial and desirable to us when prepared properly. Much of this is common sense as in the case of cooking foods which simply do not taste good or are inedible without it. While there are some who would argue that these foods should simply not be eaten, experience has shown to us, and many others, that over the long run a strictly raw diet can be limiting both nutritionally and psychologically. *A healthful diet is obtained from an abundance of fresh raw foods along with a variety of properly cooked ones.*

Many of the negative aspects associated with cooking can be avoided. The concerns and controversies regarding the undesirable effects that can occur during the heating of certain foods certainly has its justification in many cases, but more importantly are the reasons for why they occur. The saying "you are what you eat" is truly a mouthful today, and since we are ingesting more than just food in our food these days, healthy eating requires more awareness than simply following a recipe.

One such concern is the discovery of *acrylamide*, a chemical neurotoxin, mutagen, and carcinogen with the potential to accumulate in the body and cause harm. The reason for the high concern is that it is present in many foods that are consumed regularly by many people. Some of these foods contain high amounts of this toxin: chips, french fries, breads, cookies and baked goods, baby foods (including very high amounts in teething biscuits and cookies!), olives, coffee, chocolate, and more. Even simple foods that have the potential to be healthy such as grains, nuts, seeds, potatoes, sweet potatoes, winter squash, etc. can become harmful during the heating/cooked process. Acrylamide is formed by a heat induced reaction between sugar (glucose, fructose, and sucrose) and asparagines, an amino acid found in many foods and particularly high in starchy foods such as tubers and grains. The greatest accumulations of acrylamide are formed when foods containing these sugars are heated at high temperatures, as in frying, grilling, and baking. *The more food is browned and/or the longer it is cooked, the greater the amount of acrylamides formed.*

There is a growing number of this and other types of concerns occurring in our environment and food supply. While the reasons for their negative actions aren't always as simple or singular as they may appear, we can help to protect our health and our world by becoming informed and choosing to support only safe and responsible products and practices wherever concerned. These choices have a tremendous impact on our lives...for better or worse!

We can further minimize toxins and undesirable compounds found and created in our diet through proper preparation and cooking techniques. The cooking of grains, legumes, and starchy vegetables allow these foods to become much more beneficial. Although these carbohydrate rich foods were found to have the potential to create high amounts of acrylamide, it is formed only in reaction to temperatures that exceed 248° F. In the more conservative methods of steaming and boiling, in which temperatures do not exceed 212°, acrylamides are not formed.

The added methods of sprouting and fermenting grains and legumes is particularly useful in deactivating harmful and inhibiting agents including decreasing sugars and their ability to form acrylamides during the cooking process. *See Sprouting and Fermenting chapters for more information.*

During our heated quest to gain access to the goodness and digestibility we desire, we may lose some heat sensitive nutrients. This becomes most relevant when heating fruits and vegetables. The most vulnerable nutrients include many of the B vitamins, Vitamins A, C, D and E, some phytonutrients and enzymes. Most studies reveal that minerals are not affected by heat but can be leached out of food into the cooking water. The greatest losses in nutrients occur with high heat, extensive cooking times, and over cooking. Steaming or boiling, such as when making soup where the cooking liquid is also consumed, has been found to be the least destructive and the best methods for preserving nutrients.

Along with the deactivation of many undesirable compounds, the nutrients gained from the cooking of certain vegetables and all grains and legumes, lies in the softening and release of nutrients and other beneficial compounds that are bound to the cellulose structure of the food. These include carotenoids, proteins, antioxidants such as lycopene, and other phytonutrients.

Consuming a variety of raw and cooked plant foods will offer greater choice and nutrition.

Tips for retaining, preserving, and optimizing nutrients while cooking:

- Start with fresh, local, organic, and unprocessed foods to offer the most beneficial outcome.
- Overcooking is the greatest offender in nutrient loss.
- Use the color test. Colors such as red, orange, yellow, and green become more vibrant when their beneficial compounds and nutrients have been released, usually occurring within 3-7 minutes of cooking. This offers the most nutrients and least destruction. *Foods have little value left when colors are lost.*
- Avoid frying and grilling. The browning and charring of food creates carcinogenic and other forms of toxins.
- Minimize cooking temperatures, times, and browning of foods. Steaming, stewing, or boiling is best and of particular importance for high starch foods.
- B Vitamins and Vitamin C are water soluble and can be lost in cooking water. Use little or no water and short cooking times to help retain vitamins and freshness. If you do use water for cooking, try to serve with the meal or utilize in soups, sauces, etc.
- Vitamins A, D, and E are fat soluble vitamins and will leach into any oil or drippings during cooking, therefore it is best to use very little oil and utilize any drippings.
- The heating of fats and oils leads to oxidation, the creation of free radicals, trans fatty acids, and other harmful by-products. The oxidation of fats is influenced by the amount of unsaturated fats found in oils (oils liquid at room temperature) and usually have a smoke point less than 180°. *When oil begins to smoke it is a sign of oxidation and that toxins are being formed.*
- Coconut oil is high in saturated fats and is one of the most stable oils to cook with. Quality grapeseed oil is another very neutral tasting oil that can be used when cooking at higher temperatures.
- Olive oil is high in mono-saturated fats and a smoke point of about 200° F. Virgin and extra virgin olive oils also contain anti-oxidants which help resist oxidation.
- Steaming minimizes loss of nutrients, but again cook no longer than necessary.
- Leafy greens are done as soon as their color turns bright green.
- When cooking root vegetables and their tops, add stems and

greens toward the end of cooking time.
- Stewing tomatoes (with skin) at low temperatures increases the anti-oxidant Lycopene.
- Leaving skin on carrots, potatoes, and other root vegetables while cooking helps retain more nutrients.
- Only prepare enough food for one meal, leftovers should be consumed within 24 hours as refrigeration and oxidation depletes nutrients.
- Grains and legumes are more alkaline and retain certain enzymes when cooked over low heat.
- Avoid heating honey over 104° F. When heated, molecules in honey become glue like, adhering to mucous membranes and clogging the body's channels.

Common foods that become more beneficial when *properly* cooked:
Asparagus
Beets
Broccoli
Brussel Sprouts
Cabbage
Carrots
Collards
Parsley
Spinach
Winter Squash

Common foods that should always be cooked before consumption:
Most Grains
Legumes
Mushrooms
Sweet Potatoes
Potatoes
Rhubarb

With the use of proper food preparing tactics...every body wins!

Chapter 2

Anti-Nutrition

There is much excitement and concern these days surrounding substances known as "anti-nutrients". An anti-nutrient is a substance that is not necessarily toxic per se, but is unfavorable because it either inhibits digestion of certain nutrients or binds them during digestion to prevent uptake. Of special concern is the anti-nutrient *phytic acid*, found most abundantly in the bran/skin and germ portions of grains, nuts, seeds and legumes. What has been discovered about phytic acid is that it keeps the mineral phosphorus tightly bound and not readily bio-available to humans and animals with only one stomach. It also binds to other minerals such as calcium, magnesium, iron, and zinc, making them unavailable and therefore unable to perform the important task of reducing acid in the body. Additionally, enzymatic actions needed to break down proteins and starches are inhibited by the presence of phytic acid.

For century's cultures around the world who consumed grains, nuts, seeds, and legumes as dietary staples traditionally used methods of preparing these foods to increase their digestibility and nutritional value. This could include soaking, sprouting, grinding, fermenting, and cooking. Today we know through research that these methods were utilized to eliminate anti-nutrients and other toxins as well as to increase the beneficial properties contained in these foods. Somewhere down the line however, it was decided these methods were unnecessary and time consuming, instead we focused on ways of processing for the ease of convenience with little regard to the harm these foods would cause...let alone how they could possibly benefit us, hence the invention of junk food! Eating habits now revolve around fast and easy meal preparation and prepared foods that contain large concentrations of acid producing, processed, and refined foods void of health producing nutrients and alkalizing minerals. The breads, cereals, chips, snacks, and many other foods created of convenience have contributed greatly to obesity, mineral deficiencies, tooth decay, digestive and nervous disorders, and other maladies that accompany an overly acidic condition.

Similar to phytic acid is *oxalic acid*, another anti-nutrient that binds with calcium and decreases the availability of other minerals. Oxalic acid is found most abundantly in leafy greens like spinach, chard, beet greens, and in chocolate.

While it might appear that phytic and oxalic acid containing foods would best be avoided...along with many others if we looked close enough...it is important to understand that it is only in excess or when one is suffering from certain conditions that these substances become reason for concern. In fact, when the divine plan of moderation and variety is taken into consideration, these substances can be beneficial and even vital to health. Phytic acid for instance acts as an antioxidant, exhibits anti tumor/anti cancer activity, has the ability to reduce cholesterol, lower triglycerides, and offers a positive effect on the glycemic response of certain high carbohydrate foods. Oxalic acid helps cleanse the body of toxins by renewing and purifying the blood.

It is the way of nature and its ability to survive that such an array of incredible chemicals, acids, inhibitors, toxins, vitamins, minerals, enzymes, etc. all exist. The remarkable ability of human kind to survive and thrive within this balance relies on the body's ability to extract, utilize, detoxify, and eliminate properly. The method for successful and regular completion of these tasks has always consisted of fresh nutrient rich foods eaten in moderation, plenty of fresh air, pure water, exercise, Love, and of course a large helping of joy. *Also very beneficial when practiced in reverse order!*

Ok, back to the food demons!...

Since the advent of agriculture mankind has evolved more and more into a nut!, seed, grain, and legume eating species, with the law of cause and effect now causing us to look at new ways (including looking back at old ways) of coping with the abundance of potentially harmful substances that now exist in our diet. Re-establishing the traditional food preparation techniques of sprouting and fermenting, as well as cooking where appropriate, *are* necessary to reduce or eliminate excess anti-nutrients and other toxins abundant in today's food supply. Besides dramatically increasing nutritional value, the sprouting of foods neutralizes tannins and enzyme inhibitors as well as partially breaks down phytic acid. Fermentation creates foods rich in lactobacilli and other beneficial micro flora and produce the enzyme *phytase*, an enzyme that further breaks down phytic acids. Fermented foods fortify the digestive system with enzyme and pro-biotic activity helping to better process and eliminate anti-nutrients and other unwanted toxins.

Other beneficial practices include utilizing organically grown and produced foods, as commercially available foods are commonly grown with the use of high-phosphate fertilizers causing higher amounts of phytic acid to form. It has also been shown that a diet rich in vitamins A, C, and D, beta carotene, and calcium help mitigate problems as well.

A little extra effort afforded toward those foods that contain substances which work against our human bodies will enable us to bite into a wider variety of foods with greater safety and benefit.

Our Dear Friend The Body

It is often our dear friend the body that communicates the state of our physical needs and condition. Its relationship with our mental and emotional state of being is evident as well. When well, we experience sustained energy and vitality of wellness along with more clarity of mind and stability of emotions.

Physical needs are unique and individual, therefore a diet that provides nourishment and creates health will be as individual as you are. Each of our situations and needs vary and are in a continuous daily and life long state of evolvement, fluctuating to the changes occurring in our environment, season, activity, stress, age, illness, etc. *Our bodies' needs are not met within a set format of preconceived needs, and when treated as such can create much imbalance.*

The requirements and needs of the body has been an area greatly misunderstood. One of the quickest ways to increase energy and wellbeing is to eat less...of more! Today it is very typical to consume large amounts of foods while receiving very little nourishment. The needs of our body consist of the restoration of nutrients and energy that has been spent as well as required for all of its processes. The body will feel the need to eat until the gratification that comes with having these needs fulfilled are met. If not satisfied, due to lack of vitality and/or variety of foods consumed, the urge to continue eating until full, or uncomfortable, will persist. We are a society that has become accustomed to overeating—the feeling of fullness is how we have come to gauge when we have had enough. *The sensation of being full is an indicator that the digestive system is overwhelmed and food is not being processed effectively.* This process consumes a tremendous amount of energy and resources, which is why we experience symptoms of heaviness, fatigue, indigestion, etc. Of more importance are the resulting effects that continue long after the symptoms have subsided. When food is not broken down and processed in a timely manner, undigested food decays and forms toxins which the body must eliminate. Those that cannot be eliminated will be stored. Fat cells are a favorite storage unit for toxins, and the body will create more fat to accommodate more toxins as needed. Other toxic wastes will settle in the weaker and more disease prone areas of the body that do not operate efficiently enough to remove them. *You can imagine what happens when this occurs on a regular basis.*

So, besides making good food choices, it is a highly beneficial practice to avoid overeating. Allowing our digestive system to operate efficiently and completely enables the entire system to further cleanse, heal, and rejuvenate (a key factor for slowing the aging process), lessen inflammation and pain permitting the body to operate with more ease and efficiency, and eliminate toxins to reduce the creation of illness and disease.

Our body relies on us just as we rely on it, not only for survival, but for how well we survive. As you get acquainted with your body, just as you get to know a dear friend more with time, understanding your body's communication becomes clear, and your life-long companion can be nurtured. *Like all relationships you get out what you put in!*

Chapter 3

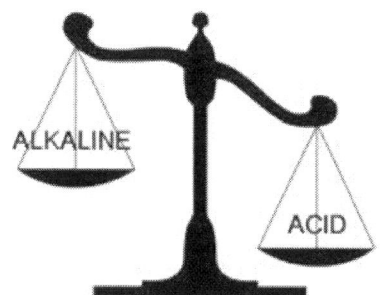

PH Connection

In this chapter we will be discussing some of the numerous implications that pH (alkaline/acid balance) has on our well-being. The importance and usefulness of this information can be of tremendous value as it addresses many of the health challenges found in our lives.

During the course of the day our bodies are in a constant state of metabolism. This process generates many acid waste products through its many routine functions and activities. This acid must be neutralized and eliminated continuously to keep the system free from its harmful effects. To achieve this we need to provide a diet consisting primarily of alkalizing foods and beverages. *Deep breathing and moderate exercise are also important processes in de-acidifying the body.* When we eat, drink, breathe, and bathe we are either nourishing the 75 trillion cells in our body or depleting, polluting, and destroying them. What we breathe, whether oxygen fortified clean air or environmental contaminants, ends up in our bloodstream. What we eat, whether living organic fruits, vegetables, nuts, grains, legumes, and seeds, or refined, processed, foodless foods, and toxic sugar laden drinks, ends up after digestion in our bloodstream. Our bloodstream is like a circulating river that both nourishes and cleanses the cells. In large part it is the foods we eat that determine if that river runs unobstructed and pure or stagnant and polluted, as well as determine the ratio of acid to alkaline elements in our bodily tissues.

What makes raw fruits, vegetables, and other living foods so vital to health is the amount of alkalizing nutrients and minerals they contain, as well as the effect they have on every cell and function in the body. When these foods are absent in the diet the body struggles to neutralize and eliminate acids within the blood. To maintain balance in the blood is first priority. When an acidic condition is present, the body is forced to relocate excess acid residues into extra-cellular fluids and connective tissue cells; this accumulation of acidic waste in the blood, cells, and organs creates internal chaos and destruction.

Initial symptoms of an overly acidic system can include foggy thinking, poor memory, headaches, depression, fatigue, muscle stiffness, poor muscle recovery, low back pain, and muscle spasms. Twitching can also occur as a result of calcium being pulled from the system to neutralize acids. If acidity increases, the body pulls even more alkalizing minerals from the system, eventually creating degenerative diseases such as arthritis, osteoporosis, cardiovascular disease, and so on. Fatigue and weakness develop from toxemia in the system as tissues and organs no longer effectively eliminate the toxins of an acidic environment...and this is just the beginning!

When the blood becomes too acidic the body's defense is to release alkalizing minerals. These minerals are generally taken from the digestive, nervous, and skeletal systems, but others will suffer as well. This depletion creates weakness and malfunctions in these systems and sets the stage for many other imbalances to occur. Because the range of a healthy blood pH is so narrow, it is very important to maintain a high reserve of alkaline mineral salts to supply the constant needs of maintaining this very delicate balance. When these reserves are exhausted the result is an accumulation of acid residues in the cells. In this acidic low oxygen environment cells die and ferment, encouraging the growth and infiltration of fungus, molds, parasites, cancer cells, etc. who seek this diseased acid waste as food. As these organisms feed, they too produce waste, which are again toxic. Being acids themselves these wastes greatly worsen an acidic condition as they spill into the blood and inside cells where they cause free radical damage and eventually death of more and more cells...the dead cells are yet another form of acid waste. Blood poisoning results in more cells and tissues and further growth of morbid forms of yeast, molds, and viruses form to disrupt body chemistry and cause disease to the systems. *One acidic condition creates another and another to form a truly vicious cycle!* It is not bacteria or viruses themselves that produce disease; it is the acidic by-products of microorganisms acting upon the unbalanced malfunctioning cell metabolism that produces disease. It is these now common acidic conditions of our population that are the largest underlying causes of cancer, heart disease, arteriosclerosis, high blood pressure, diabetes, arthritis, gout, kidney disease, asthma, allergies, psoriasis and other skin disorders, etc. *Normal cells cannot survive in a low oxygen acidic environment, cancer cells and other unwanted microorganisms however, thrive in it!*

While there are a number of causes that contribute to an overly acidic condition, such as stress, negative emotions, poor environmental conditions, and other lifestyle factors, the most common cause and cure can be found through diet. By restoring a balanced pH and maintaining an alkaline mineral reserve we can safeguard our health and even reverse the disease process.

The main factor that determines whether a food is acid or alkaline forming is the type and amount of minerals it contains.

Calcium, magnesium, sodium, potassium, and iron are the primary alkalinizing minerals. Foods that are higher in sulfur, phosphorus, iodine, and chlorine are acid forming foods. Many natural foods will contain both alkaline and acid forming minerals; whichever is the higher concentration will determine which end of the spectrum it falls. Most all *ripe* fruits and vegetables are alkalizing. Commercially grown fruits and vegetables may be less alkalizing due to growing conditions, mineral-depleted soil, and picking while unripe. Generally, the more natural sugars that develop in a fruit or vegetable the riper it is and the more alkaline forming it will be. Proteins, particularly cooked flesh foods, are very acidifying. Most fats, especially cooked fats, are acid forming, not only because of the toxins created in the heating process, but also because they tend to clog the arteries which affect circulation and oxygen, creating increased cell toxicity and cell death. Synthetic foods, additives, colorings, preservatives, etc. are all acidic. Processed foods, soft drinks, alcohol, coffee, and all synthetic vitamins and prescription drugs are *extremely* acidic. Balancing alkaline forming foods with acid forming ones in proper proportions is key to creating and maintaining proper pH in the body. Research has found that the optimal intake ratio of alkaline to acid forming food is approximately 80% alkaline forming and 20% acid forming. *This is a general guideline, as there may be some individual variances.* This ratio or balance can best be achieved and sustained with a diet consisting of predominantly high mineral high water content fresh organic fruits, vegetables, soaked nuts, seeds, and legumes.

Assessing your own pH— Measuring the body's pH can be a valuable tool since it is a measurement that communicates how the body is reacting to the foods and beverages it consumes as well as the lifestyle, stress, exercise, thoughts, etc. that it is subjected to. The method for testing bodily pH that we will be discussing offers the most accuracy and benefit when used frequently over a period of weeks or even months, helping to develop more awareness and familiarity with bodily rhythms and responses. *This knowledge will help to identify where changes need to be made and offer insight as to how to refine and/or shift your diet toward a healthier more balanced state.* PH level of bodily fluids fluctuate throughout the day and are dependent on activities such as eating, exercise, stress levels, etc., therefore averaging the results from urine tests taken throughout a 24 hour period is needed for accuracy. This entails the use of pH test paper (available at health food stores and online). Test each urination over a 24 hour period, starting with the second urine of the day to the first urine of the following morning. While pH readings can very significantly throughout the day (generally lowest in morning and highest in evening) the averages of your 24 hour tests when compared over a matter of days, weeks, or months will be what provides the most accurate assessment of your pH. A healthy pH range (over 24 hr. period) will fluctuate between 6.3-7.2. *You may occasionally see a very high* *reading (above 8.0), most often this will not mean you are highly alkalized, it is a sign that the body is in an acidic state and has pulled alkalizing minerals from the system to neutralize the condition. This is bound to happen periodically, in fact you may notice it quite a bit at first, do not be alarmed...you are armed and in control!* Keep a running log of your diet and activities along with pH readings and use as a guide to find where improvements need to be made. The readings will let you know when you have successfully removed the offender or offenders, and soon you will simply recognize your bodies symptoms and signals without the need of p......H testing!

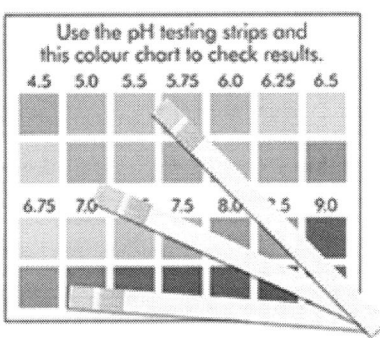

Saliva pH is an indicator of the amount of alkaline reserves in the body and the condition of the pH of the cells. A normal pH taken in the morning and before meals is 6.8-7.2. Clinical research indicates that if the morning saliva pH (upon rising) is below 6.2, it suggests an acidic system with inadequate alkaline minerals but with some alkaline reserves. If the saliva pH is below 5.8 with no rise after a meal, it means the body is acidic with no alkaline reserves. *Building mineral reserves is your goal and will improve over time as you adopt a more alkaline forming diet.* Testing your pH is a helpful tool, but aside from what your readings may say, when your body becomes balanced you will recognize good energy levels, a clear mind, more joy, less anger and irritability, better digestion and elimination, less symptoms of illness and pain, and an overall feeling of vitality and wellness.

Chapter 4

The Power of Green

Hope you aren't silly enough to think we're referring to green, as in moola, denaro, or the cold hard stuff. Indeed not, in this chapter we're referring to the far more powerful head of lettuce and its relatives.

While virtually all vegetables, regardless of shape, size, or color are beneficial to health in numerous ways, it is the green leafy ones that rein supreme. One reason is chlorophyll, the blood supply of green plants that's loaded with nutrients such as protein, vitamins A, C, and D, vital minerals like magnesium, and many others. Since chlorophyll is so molecularly similar to human blood, these nutrients are fully assimilated by us. Chlorophyll also facilitates our oxygen uptake strengthening our defenses against environmental pollutants and upgrading our cellular resistance to most or all forms of degeneration.

Leafy greens are also some of the best foods for reducing inflammation and acidity in the body. When consumed with other foods, especially acid forming ones like grains, legumes, pasteurized dairy, and meats, leafy greens begin working immediately to help control the many harmful effects these foods can cause. When consumed regularly leafy greens boost the body's alkaline mineral reserves to help neutralize acidity before damage can occur.

Edible green leafy vegetation includes prized and cared for ones like kale, chard, spinach, arugula, mustard greens, lettuces, and home grown green sprouts like broccoli and sunflower greens, as well as wild growing ones like dandelion, chick weed, nettle, miners lettuce, watercress, and many more. Edible seaweed and algae like kelp, dulse, kombu, chlorella, and spirulina are also super green foods that can add a whole new spectrum of nutrients.

Leafy greens combine well with most all other foods in regards to digestion and taste. Besides counteracting the negative or harmful effects when consumed *with* lesser quality foods, they also make for an effective antidote when consumed *after* over indulgence of other less than favorable foods like sweets, caffeine, or alcohol.

So...if by choice or chance of fate you happen to overdo...of cookies or cake or some other mistake...or maybe even of two, too late to turn back...with Rolaids there's lack, feel free to try this tip instead, a heaping of kelp or kale is more help...than any tablet, prescription, or med, so less is the cost and health that is lost, and less is the damage that's done, but better yet still...exercise your free will, no need to miss out on the fun, it's "Healthy Junk"...where health and satisfaction are one!

An easy and convenient way of consuming any variety of leafy greens is by way of a salad. Beneficial bitter, spicy, or bland greens that would otherwise not make it to the table can be combined with more neutral tasting varieties to enhance both taste and nutrition. *Often we end up with such a mix of greens, from garden lettuces and garlic tops to wild foraged greens, we never know what to expect...but are seldom disappointed!*

Growing or foraging for greens and eating them soon after harvest is most optimal as it offers the greatest benefits to health. Next to this, and available to most of us for at least a portion of the year, is shopping at a local farmers market for fresh organically grown greens. However, if it is through swinging by your local grocery store and purchasing organic pre-washed ready-to-go salad greens that helps to increase your intake of this very essential ingredient...that's perfect!

One method of convenience that we have discovered useful on occasion is to acquire a variety of greens (preferably from a local farmers market) in enough of a quantity to last for several days, hose the heads or bunches off one at a time, give them a good shaking to get as much water off as possible, tear them into bite size pieces by hand, throw them all together in a large plastic bag with some dry paper towels, and refrigerate. *Using fresh greens, tearing instead of cutting with a metal knife, and adding paper towel to absorb water, all help to extend freshness.*

Another method of convenience that we have come to appreciate as well as *thoroughly* enjoy, is to blend and drink our salad...hey don't knock it till you give it a whirl! A blended salad can provide a quick, alkalizing, and easily digestible pick me up and/or hold over. Besides eliminating the need for salad dressing, receive even more benefit by adding a fermented liquid like rejuvelac, beet kvass, etc. See *Green Light* recipe in "Beverages" for ideas.

Did you know, of the four main types of lettuce: leaf lettuce, crisphead (i.e. iceberg), romaine, and bibb, that leaf lettuce is the most nutritious. This is because the arrangement of its leaves, being loose and exposed to the sun, cause it to create protective antioxidant sunscreens in shades of red, purple, or reddish brown. In turn we receive this UV protection when we consume them. *The inner leaves of crisphead lettuces contain only 1% the antioxidants of leaf lettuce.*

The most important task when consuming a green salad is to CHEW WELL! Even though we have strong digestive fluids, thoroughly chewing to break down the tough cellulose membranes that coat and protect leafy greens must precede digestion in order to effectively extract and make use of vital nutrients housed within.

Salad...it's what should be for dinner!

Besides calming our body and mind by neutralizing the effects of less desirable foods that we may have eaten, or will be eating, a salad *containing greens as its majority* will digest quickly, leaving our body with little to do but rest and repair itself during our nightly slumber. And since lettuce is related to the opium poppy it contains a natural sedative which helps us get to sleep faster and sleep sounder.

Dressing to impress:

If salads haven't impressed you much in the past you probably haven't dressed them properly. Dressing can be like icing on the cake, and for many of us the difference whether we will even eat a salad or not. The trick of course is finding a dressing as desirable as icing, but with a better cast of ingredients. Many commercially produced salad dressings consist of low–quality oils stripped of their nutrients and made dangerously rancid by high temperature or solvent extraction processes, poor quality vinegars, refined sugars, and other non-food items like stabilizers, preservatives, artificial flavors, and colors...all of which work against the reason why we would want to eat salad in the first place! You will be thrilled to know however, that making your own tasty and healthy salad dressing is a piece of cake...with icing of course!

The main and quite likely most important ingredient in salad dressing is the fat or oil that it contains. Not only do good quality fats and oils provide important nutrients in and of themselves, but when combined with greens work synergistically to utilize nutrients in greens that would otherwise stay locked up. Taste and ability to coat are other attributes that are also hard to match without oils flavor and viscosity. The problem with most oils is that they self destruct very quickly after being separated from their source. Even the best methods of extraction can render oils anywhere from nutritionally void to dangerously rancid.

A *high quality* **extra virgin olive oil** is a good choice for salad dressings. High quality olive oil will be unfiltered—cloudy, and will be golden yellow in color—a sign that it has been pressed from ripe olives. *High quality olive oil still contains its original content of antioxidants which protect the oils fatty acids from rancidity. For preservation of* *nutrients, keep olive oil refrigerated...it only takes a few minutes on a counter top to become liquid.*

Another option is to use whole foods as a fat/oil source in salad dressings. Whole black (ripe) olives that have been naturally cured (not canned), avocado, toasted sesame seeds, pine nuts, and others are all good choices for adding beneficial fats while eliminating refined oils.

The other key ingredient in salad dressing and capable of enhancing both nutrition and taste is vinegar and other ferments. Ferments have the ability to enhance nutritive and digestive benefits while imparting unique flavors (i.e. sour & salty). The best types of vinegar are organic, naturally brewed, unfiltered and un-pasteurized. *Distilled vinegar should not be used as it is highly de-mineralizing.* Ferments such as rejuvelac, kvass, sauerkraut, kimchee, Nama Shoyu, miso, etc. can add desirable taste, and some of these a rich salty taste as well...which eliminates the need for additional salt.

Some additional ingredients that can augment taste and nutrition even further are fresh **ginger, turmeric, garlic, herbs & spices, nutritional yeast,** and **dried seaweeds.**

With the right ingredients and some experimenting on your own you'll be able to create an endless variety of easy, healthy, and tasty dressings that will help keep you *rolling in the green!*

We hope that you now understand the true meaning of the *power of green,* besides, with health, who needs the other green stuff anyway!

Go with the Flow

The synchronicity of nature in its many facets and forms is beyond inspiring! When left to its own devises, the nature that is life flows perfectly and in continuous accord with its environment and its sole purpose...SURVIVAL!

As human beings we are the only species on the planet able to over-ride instinct and have the capacity for free-will. Our free will gives us the ability to create a world filled with enormous variety in our life. In fact it may just be this free wheel that ran over our instinct! We have managed to create the remarkable and discover the extraordinary, but our own health and well-being continues to elude us...have we lost our senses?

The wise ancient philosophies of Ayurveda and Chinese Medicine are based and obtained through the study and observation of nature, its cycles, and principles of cause and effect. Within the body the most common cause of dysfunction, disease, and disharmony are the result of imbalances created through excessive and/or deficient amounts of elements needed to maintain balance (this applies to all levels of existence). All foods contain a combination of these essential elements (vitamins, minerals, fats, proteins and so much more...), which in turn contain the inherent properties necessary to create and allow specific actions to occur in the body. The knowledge of the properties of foods and the understanding of their actions is the key for using food as thy medicine. It accounts for the reason why no one diet works for everyone or everywhere, why special diets that create health and healing for some may create imbalance for others, and why too much of a good thing is always going to be just that...too much!

In today's world we can eat just about any variety of food at any time of the year almost anywhere. The road to civilization has paved over much of the path of nature and many of us have simply forgotten its ways. To regain the balance, health, and vitality that was given to us, we must revisit the flow of Mother Nature. This flow includes the synchronicity between our body's intrinsic needs and that which nature provides both seasonally and geographically. Its synchronicity can be observed in her offerings. Summer and hot climates are met with light, cooling, and hydrating fruits and vegetables that balance our need to replenish fluids and minerals. Fall, with its dry and increasingly cool weather, our needs for warming and moistening foods are met with complex carbohydrates like starchy winter squash, root vegetables, grains, and plant based fats such as avocados, olives, nuts and seeds...which also just so happen to store well to keep us fed during the cold dormant season of winter. The wet months of spring that signal the body's natural cycle to cleanse and transition out of the heavy foods of winter are met with leafy greens and astringent fruits which prepare us for the lighter and more active months of spring and summer.

Maintaining balance is part of our inherent nature, and if we follow her design we naturally maintain our health...subsequently, we contribute to the health of the planet through supporting seasonally fresh, local, and environmentally friendly produce and products as well.

So why not *go with the flow!*

Chapter 5

Sprouting

With a soak I'm a sprout...
"I'm alive, let me out!"
I will nourish and protect,
this and more you can expect.
from a nut or a seed, a grain or a bean,
I will treat you well and be kind to your cells,
none is more giving...
than that which is living!
       —Kim

  Sprouting is the simplest and most sustainable form of growing food in the world. It requires less care, equipment, space, and natural resources than any other method of growing food. It has no need for fertilizers or pesticides, is virtually unaffected by weather, has the fastest germination to table time, and to top it all off the resulting sprouts are some of the most nutritious foods one could ever hope to consume.

  Sprouting brings seeds, nuts, grains, and legumes out of hibernation and gives them life, turning dry dormant carbohydrates into living foods. It is the equivalent of allowing fruits and vegetables to ripen before consumption, in both cases enzymes activate to liberate valuable nutrients, molecular changes occur that enhance digestion instead of preventing it (i.e. gas from un-sprouted legumes), and become more flavorful as well as safer to consume.

  What follows is an overview of the sprouting/germination process to provide an understanding of how it all works, why it's worthwhile, and even why in many instances that it is quite necessary. After the overview more specific information will be provided about the various sprouting processes for seeds, nuts, grains, and legumes.

Sprouting Overview:

Sprouting is the birth process that all plants go through, the most edible and viable of these species are the ones that have been wisely chosen for consumption and include various tree nuts, seeds, grains, and legumes. The first requirement for sprouting is to start with viable seeds. *Purchasing seeds specifically for sprouting usually insures that this happens.* If sprouting does not occur it's because the seed and/or its life force (enzymes) have been damaged or destroyed. This could be a result of irradiation, excessive heat (including steam pasteurization), chemical spraying (also a common pasteurization process), too old (rancid), or physically broken or damaged. Once we have our prospective seedlings that meet the minimum qualifications of *being alive,* all that is needed to coax them out of hibernation is what all life requires...water! A good soaking signals the go ahead to break down and release enzyme inhibitors that have been preventing them from sprouting prematurely. While the soaking process allows certain enzyme inhibitors to be relieved of their duties, it initiates others to begin theirs. Growth enzymes ignite life force and break down stored substrates within to nourish and provide fuel for growth toward becoming a full fledged plant or tree.

All soakings need to end with the important task of thoroughly rinsing the newborns. This is done almost exclusively for our benefit since it will now be the rinse water that contains the enzyme inhibitors as well as other undesirable elements and waste products.

Once rinsed all seedlings require from here on out is periodic watering to keep them from drying out, and sunlight toward the end of their growth if they are of the greening variety. *Nuts are at the end of their germinating potential after they have been soaked, rinsed, and allowed to sit out and dry for the day.*

Through the process of germination, proteins, fats, and carbohydrates convert into easier to digest molecules like amino acids, fatty acids, and simpler carbohydrates. Since this is the same work that our digestive system performs, consuming sprouts is like consuming foods that have been pre-digested for us...think momma bird feeding baby bird! *When we eat easily digestible live foods with living enzymes like sprouts, we free up energy for other important metabolic processes.*

Sprouting Guide

Nuts:

Almonds, Brazil Nuts, Hazel Nuts, Pecans, Walnuts:
Soak 12-18 hours, rinse, and sprout no more than 1 day.

Pine Nuts, Pistachios, Macadamia Nuts:
Do not require soaking or sprouting.

Seeds:

Sunflower (hulled) and Pumpkin:
Soak 8-12 hours, rinse, and sprout 1-2 days.

Sesame (hulled or un-hulled):
Soak 8-12 hours, rinse, and sprout 1-2 days.

Sunflower (un-hulled):
See following section on "Growing Sunflower Greens".

Flax & Chia:
See following section on "Sprouting Flax & Chia Seeds".

Broccoli, Cabbage, Mustard, Onion, Radish (greening seeds):
Soak 8-12 hrs., rinse, sprout 5-6 days (last days in indirect sunlight).

Grains:

Amaranth, Buckwheat, Millet, Quinoa:
Soak 12-18 hours, rinse, and sprout 1-2 days.

Corn and Rice:
Soak 12-18 hours, rinse, and sprout 2-3 days.

Oats:
Soak 12-18 hours, rinse, and sprout no more than 1 day.

Wheat, Rye, and Barley:
See following section "Growing Wheat & Barley Grass for Juicing".

Legumes:

Adzuki, Black, Red, Garbanzos, and **Mung Beans, Lentils, etc.:**
Soak 18-24 hours, rinse, and sprout 3-5 days.

Sprouting Supplies

The following supplies allow the sprouting of all sprouts found in our recipes and more.

For jar method of sprouting: Quart size and half gallon size glass jars with screened lids to fit, or use mesh cloth with a rubber band.

For sprouting flax and chia seeds: 2 Terra Cotta saucers. *Saucers from China may contain lead so use ones from Italy or elsewhere.*

For growing sunflower greens: 3 dinner size plates and organic top soil.

For growing wheat grass or barley grass for juicing: 3+ gardening flats (plastic mesh bottom trays found at nurseries), equal amounts of organic compost & organic top soil, and newspapers.

Jar Method Sprouting Instructions

The following technique for sprouting works for virtually all seeds, nuts, grains, and legumes:

1) **Soak** - Using the appropriate size glass jar (based on quantity and anticipated size of full grown sprouts), place desired amount of raw nuts, seeds, grains, or legumes inside with twice or more the amount of pure (un-chlorinated) water. Cover with a screen lid or mesh cloth held with a rubber band and soak seeds for 8-12 hours, nuts and grains for 12-18 hours, and legumes for 18-24 hours. When soaking longer than 12 hours try to rinse and refill with fresh water about half way through. *Mix and match anything together in the same jar as long as they have roughly the same soak and germination time and you plan to use them together.*

2) **Rinse** - After soaking, pour off water through screen or mesh top followed by several rinses. Allow sprouts to drain off excess water by placing jar upside down in sink or dish rack for several minutes, then set jar in a safe well ventilated area at room temperature out of direct sunlight. *Keeping sprouts in the dark is not necessary.*

3) **Water** - From here on out you will simply need to provide your crop with regular watering by rinsing then draining like you did after their soak. Once in the morning and again at night usually suffices in most climates, but if yours is hot and dry they may also need a midday watering. If your climate is humid in addition to hot, mold may grow on the sprouts so more thorough and frequent rinsing may be needed, and/or spray with a 3% food-grade hydrogen peroxide. A fan providing air circulation can also help.

4) **Wait & Watch** - As your sprouts grow you should see tails develop...unless their nuts! Some will grow fast and long while others will grow slow and stay rather short. At any rate most sprouts will be ready for use in 2-4 days.

5) **Eat or Store** - Sprouts eventually require soil to continue growing so they do have a shelf life, or in this case a jar life, so they will need to be consumed or stored at some point before they parish (i.e. wither, spoil, smell off, etc.).
Refrigeration can be used to slow the growth of sprouts at anytime or to store them at the peak of maturity for another several days to a week. *Allow sprouts to dry thoroughly before refrigeration and leave sprouting lid on jar (instead of replacing with an air tight one) to minimize deterioration.*
Dehydration can be used for all sprouted nuts, hulled and non-leafing/non-greening sprouted seeds like sunflower and pumpkin, most sprouted grains, and even sprouted legumes if desired. Dehydration significantly extends the shelf life of sprouted foods from less to a week to several months. Dehydration can enhance the taste and digestibility of foods as well as provide readily available snacks or on hand ingredients like sprouted grains. Dehydrate at 110°-115° until desired result is achieved.

Sprouting Flax & Chia Seeds

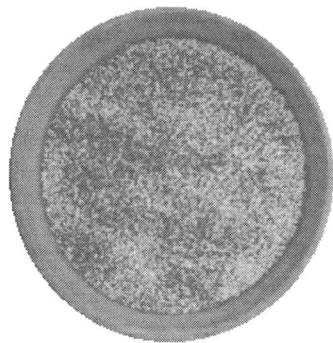

Not only are both flax and chia seeds excellent forms of beneficial fat, especially the all important omega 3's, but when consumed whole and germinated, provide nutrients beyond that of any extracted fat source, including their own oil.

Since flax and chia seeds create excess mucilage when wet, soaking them in a jar and trying to rinse them through a screen lid becomes difficult. Sprouting in a thin layer on a terra cotta saucer is a much better option, here's how to do it:

- Start with a 12" round terra cotta saucer, these can be found at most places that sell pots for planting. *Get two and make sure they are not made in China as they may contain lead; Italian made or elsewhere should be fine.*
- Cover bottom of saucer with 1/8" of pure (un-chlorinated) water.
- Sprinkle about 1/4 c *brown* flax seed (golden flax seeds bitter quickly when sprouted and are not recommended), chia seeds, or a mix of the two evenly over the water and set the saucer in a level spot anywhere out of direct sunlight.
- In mornings and evenings moisten seeds by filling saucer with a bit of water then pouring off excess (seeds will stick to saucer at this point). *Midday watering may be needed in hot and/or dry climates.*

Seeds can be used after about 8 hrs. by scraping off desired amount with a hard wood or plastic spatula. Continue harvesting for several days. Eventually they will leaf out and green, at which point they tend to become bitter, but can still be used beneficially...if desired. *The whole saucer of sprouts can be placed in fridge to stop growth and/or the progression of bitterness as well as to extend shelf life at any time.*

After use, saucers need to be cleaned and *thoroughly* dried. Fill and let saucer sit for 5 minutes with hot water. Then with the use of a stiff brush, scrub well under hot running water (no soap). Allow to dry by either placing in direct sunlight, setting on a wood burning stove, in front of a furnace, etc. *Use second saucer to start new batch of seeds while first one dries.*

If seeds start to grow mold at any time, it could be due to a contaminated saucer (that may not have dried thoroughly enough). Sterilize saucer using high heat or a diluted food grade hydrogen peroxide solution, or both. If this doesn't work get a new one. *Bad seeds may also cause mold, but is less common.*

Growing Sunflower Greens

Growing sunflower greens involves using *un-hulled* "black oil" sunflower seeds planted in soil. Start by soaking ¼ cup seeds for 8-12 hours, pack about ½" of organic soil on a dinner size plate or tray, spread soaked seeds evenly over soil and water well, use a second plate or tray and place upside down on top of the first. While holding plates together, tip sidewise in a sink and allow excess water to drain, place as is in a safe location at room temperature. After 3 days remove top plate, soak soil and seeds and drain as before with the use of second plate, remove top plate and place sprouts where they will receive an ample amount of indirect sunlight. *For consecutive sprouting start another batch of seeds at this time...or earlier!* From now on simply keep soil moist (not soggy) by saturating soil then tipping to drain off excess water. *Besides watering, spraying/misting sprout tops with a spray bottle will allow shells to fall off and/or be removed easier.* Sprouts can be harvested when they reach about 3" and green up by cutting close to the soil with scissors, serrated knife, or a pinch of the fingertips, the later of which is kid friendly!

Sunflower sprouts are high in fiber, protein (24-30%, including 8 essential amino acids), essential fatty acids, and vitamins A, B complex (including B12 & B15), C, D, and E. They also contain calcium, phosphorous, iron, iodine, potassium, magnesium, and the trace elements zinc, manganese, copper and chromium.

Growing Wheat & Barley Grass for Juicing

While wheat and barley are used in everything from bread to...well most everything, in this book we only use them to grow grass for juicing. When only the grass of these grains are used (completely void of seed) there is *no* gluten content for the first 10-14 days of growth. Beyond this, "jointing" or the development of gluten within the grass occurs. *Consuming before 10 days is usually not an issue, especially if not allowing to re-grow for a second cutting (not recommended anyway).*

Grass juices are true "super foods" as they are highly alkalizing, mineralizing, energizing, and much more, making them well worth the effort, here's how:

First off, a wheat grass juicer specifically designed for extracting juice from grasses will be needed. Expense is dependent on which version and how many bells and whistles you would like. A manual hand crank version will be cheaper and probably last longer, but most people opt for some form of an electrical version for convenience.

Once you have a juicer the following items are all that are needed for growing your own grasses:
- **Hard red winter wheat berries** and/or **barley grains**.
- 2+ **gardening flats** (mesh bottom plastic trays). *16" square tray yields about 16 oz. of juice.*
- Equal amounts of **organic compost** and **organic top soil**.
- **Newspapers**.

Directions for growing and juicing grasses:

1) Soak 1½ cups of desired grain for 8-12 hours in a sprouting jar with a mesh or screen lid. *We use 1 cup wheat berries and 1/2 cup barley and add 1 tsp. liquid kelp to get grains off to a good start.*
2) Drain and sprout 24-36 hrs. (tails well formed). *Use soak water to water plants.*
3) Cover mesh bottom of gardening flat with a single layer of newspaper.
4) Pre-mix equal amounts of compost and top soil, fill tray with about 1" of the mix.
5) Water soil making sure it is completely saturated.
6) Spread seeds over moistened soil and water again.
7) Loosely cover with dark plastic. When sprouts are about 1" high remove plastic and place tray in indirect sunlight in well ventilated area, using fan if necessary.
8) Soil needs to be kept moist but not soggy, this usually entails watering every to every other day depending on weather conditions.

If mold forms at the base of grass it is caused by the lack of air circulation (use fan) and/or too much water. Temperatures between 65° and 85° are preferable.

Start harvesting and juicing wheat grass when it gets 6" high, barley grass when it gets 3-4" high, by grabbing a handful of grass and with the use of a serrated knife cutting as close to soil as possible. Juice and drink immediately...but slowly!

When first introducing grass juices to your diet it is recommended to start with ½ oz. and work up to 2 oz. one or more times a day, depending on physical condition (those fighting cancer and other disease might want more) and/or desired results.

<u>Healthy Junk Sprout Picks & misc. Sprout Info</u>

Nuts—

Because shelled nuts are not capable of germinating beyond their soak, and in fact have been set on a short course of existence because of it, they need to be either consumed from their jar within two days, allowed to air dry and stored in the fridge (preferably with a breathable lid) and then consumed within the week, or be dehydrated for longer term storage.

Since nuts show no visible signs of sprouting it can be difficult to know if they were healthy nuts in the first place. To ensure quality specimens and avoid rancidity, toxins, radiation, etc. acquire raw organic and unshelled (whenever practical) nuts from the current years harvest. *If nuts (shelled) float in soak water, they are rancid.*

Almonds are the most alkalizing and arguably the most nutritious of all nuts, this along with their versatility makes them the most commonly found in our recipes.

Since 2007 federal law, through the Almond Board of California (ABC), states that for "safety reasons" almonds grown in California (most U.S. almonds are) must be sterilized by pasteurization or irradiation prior to shipping anywhere in North America. This means unless you go to the farmer (i.e. farmers market) and buy them direct, the almonds you end up with have been subjected to, but not limited to, steam, oil or dry roasting, blanching, chemical spraying with Propylene Oxide (PPO), or irradiation. Since steam treatment and chemical spraying are both said to be "surface treatments" that do not effect the viability of nuts (they still sprout), the FDA allows them to be labeled as a "raw" product. The FDA and ABC claim that government research findings and independent expert lab analyses of pasteurized almonds has found "no degradation of taste, quality or nutritional value of treated almonds (regardless of method)". Other independent experts (including the EPA) and their lab analyses however, paint a more toxic picture. They summarize that PPO, a volatile liquid initially created for making plastics, is a verified carcinogenic responsible for neurological, gastrointestinal, respiratory, immune system dysfunctions, and liver disease. Even more telling than the EU, Canada, and Mexico banning PPO due to known carcinogenic risk to humans, is the US National Hot Rod Association banning its use as a *fuel additive*...because the fumes were too toxic!

Irradiation is another form of "making foods safe" that has been shown to damage or destroy cells and DNA, increasing health risks like cancer and death. While PPO appears to be the poison of choice for almonds, irradiation is not off the table. Even raw almonds from foreign countries, brought in by demand for a healthier choice, are capable of being irradiated at the discretion of US Customs.

What follows, in order of significance, are the criteria we have found most helpful in obtaining not only quality, but safe almonds:

1) **Buy raw almonds direct from farmer.** Domestic almonds that have not received any form of pasteurization are usually only available when in season and directly from a farmer in California who grows them. *The domestic almonds you see labeled as "raw" in health food stores and elsewhere have been pasteurized!* Buying directly from a reputable farmer is not only the best option for truly raw, non-pasteurized, and non-irradiated almonds, but usually the most economical as well, especially when buying in bulk. *The USDA only allows small scale farmers to sell raw almonds in small quantities from "roadside" events under the condition that they do not claim their crop to be any better (raw, organically grown, etc.) than conventionally grown almonds, based on the idea they will have an "unfair advantage" over their competition. So whether a farmer talks or not, buying direct is still likely to be your best bet.*

2) ***Buy organic almonds.*** Although store bought organic domestic almonds have been pasteurized, it is a steam pasteurization process and not the dangerous PPO chemical treatment that many conventional almonds receive. Also any food declared as organic is spared the harmful practice of irradiation. Steam pasteurization is of course heat, which can and will destroy some or all nutrients in food, depending on intensity and duration, but compared to the toxic alternative, buying organic gives far less reasons for panic.

3) ***Buy non-local.*** The EU *does not* allow GMO products and *does* allow almonds to be sold un-pasteurized. Their almonds are also of an heirloom variety, which usually means they are a more beneficial variety than hybrids, like those grown in the states. Their only downfall, besides obviously not being local, is that U.S. Customs has discretion over irradiating them before they ever get to the U.S. market place. This *should not* apply if almonds are labeled "organic" however, and if you trust your supplier they will know if their shipment was irradiated because customs will advise them that it was required...and make them pay for it.

4) ***Buy a sample, soak and try.*** When you cannot get almonds in any of the above listed ways, or if you want to validate the claims of almond suppliers who do make any of the above claims, you can perform a simple experiment. What we have found, through trial and error, accurately determines the quality of almonds is to examine the water in which they have received their 12+ hour soak in. *Purity of soak water indicates the purity and freshness of almonds soaking in it, the more polluted the water looks and/or smells, the older and /or more polluted and/or toxic the almonds are.* It's ok for the water to turn a translucent brown as this is only tannins from the skins that we want washed away anyway, but if the water is cloudy white and/or otherwise murky, it may be an indication that the almonds are of poor quality. *Quality being defined as fresh, alive, and without chemicals.* Another clue is that after sprouting, poor quality almonds will display virtually no shelf life. Our senses can also aid in quality control before our purchase. Fresh domestic almonds look firm, plump, and almost glow, while the European heirloom variety is more flat and dense. Both should smell and taste fresh, sweet, and have a good crunch.

    Walnuts & Pecans are two other popular nuts found in our recipes. Obtaining these with shells intact, whenever possible and practical, ensures freshness and better chance of avoiding irradiation and chemical treatment. *The California Walnut Board's website lays out the "Standard Operating Procedure for Pasteurization of Walnuts" which involves the same dangerous PPO chemical pasteurizing technique administered to un-shelled almonds.* So without having to verbally beat these nuts to death, like we had to with almonds, let's just say we highly recommend buying un-shelled nuts, preferably organic.

Macadamia and **pine nuts** contain low levels of phytates making it not necessary to soak/sprout these nuts.

Pistachios while high enough in phytate to justify sprouting, tend to mold easily, so un-sprouted and in moderation is our advise on these.

Brazil Nuts are very high in phyate and should be soaked and preferably dehydrated prior to use, especially when consumed regularly.

Seeds—

Sprouts from *hulled* seeds like pumpkin and sunflower do grow a bit of a tail when sprouted, but like nuts stop growing as soon as they figure out they have no protective shell. These seed sprouts tend to bitter quickly and are best consumed within a day or two after their soak. *Storing in fridge adds a few days.*

Sprouts from *un-hulled* seeds like broccoli, cabbage, radish, and onion are meant to be grown into full size (1-3 inch) sprouts and "greened up". *This can all be accomplished with the jar method.*

Because of longer germination time, greening sprouts need good airflow. Keep jar in a well ventilated area right side up or on its side (as apposed to upside down in dish rack) to allow air in through screen or mesh cover. Continue watering and rinsing like any other sprout. As leaves form place in *indirect* sunlight to continue growth and for the development of chlorophyll. Start using as soon as sprouts start turning a darker green. If not consumed within a few days of greening, store in fridge (preferably when not too wet) with breathable lid intact, and use within 4-5 days. In hotter weather (85°+) broccoli sprouts and other "cool weather crops" deteriorate quickly, so will need to be stored and used from fridge as soon as they mature and green up.

Some seed sprouts used in our recipes include **broccoli, brown & black un-hulled sesame seeds, hulled pumpkin, hulled & un-hulled sunflower, flax and chia seeds.** *Seeds more commonly known and used as grains, such as millet, amaranth, and buckwheat are covered under grains.* Other recommended seed sprouts are **onion, brown mustard, radish,** and **cabbage seeds. Alfalfa** and **clover** sprouts are actually legumes and contain the natural occurring protective substance *canavanine* during the early stages of sprouting and are best not consumed until fully mature (a minimum of 5 days of germination; leafed out and greened).

Grains—

Like nuts, seeds, and legumes, grains are high in the anti-nutrient phytic acid, and because grains dominate our modern day diet, it is especially healthful that they be sprouted prior to consumption.

Besides phytic acid, grains like wheat, rye and barley also contain the more familiar substance gluten, which for some (including those who may not know it) cause health issues ranging anywhere from mild to extreme.

It is with ultimate health for all in mind that we not only recommend such methods as sprouting, dehydrating, fermenting, and in some cases cooking to render offending foods more beneficial and less harmful, but that we use only gluten free grains as well (except wheat & barley which are used in growing grasses). These include **corn, rice, millet, amaranth, oats,** and **buckwheat.** Others to try are **sorghum, teff,** and **quinoa.** *If you wish to use glutinous grains like wheat, rye and barley, the sprouting process is the same.*

The once nutritious **corn** has become an extensively hybridized, genetically modified, highly refined, and excessively used grain that now causes hypersensitivity issues for many. *This new version of corn is no longer a beneficial food.* With this said organic (non-GMO) less hybridized corn can be acquired to both nourish and provide diversity in the diet. Quality dried whole kernel corn sprouts easily, and along with fermentation can create a delicious and more valuable food source. *See "Resources" for quality suppliers of dried "whole kernel corn" for sprouting.*

While the East has remedied the high consumption of anti-nutrients in their staple food of rice by removing its germ and bran, it is at the cost of lost nutrients. Sprouting remedies this issue as well, but while allowing consumption of the whole food with all of its benefit. *The refinement of brown rice into white rice removes 60-90% of many of its nutrients and all of its fiber and essential fatty acids. Brown rice is the only grain that contains vitamin E, but is completely destroyed when refined.* Not all rice available is of sufficient quality to sprout. Rice must be un-refined (germ and bran intact), so this excludes any rice with "white" as part of its name and most rice that does not have "brown" in its name. The following are varieties of rice that should sprout well when purchased from a quality supplier: **short grain brown rice, sweet rice, brown basmati, brown jasmine, red thai** and **wehani.** *Wild Rice is not rice, it is also incapable of sprouting.*

Millet, amaranth, buckwheat and **quinoa** are seed grains fast to sprout. The hardier millet and quinoa are good choices to top salads, use in pilafs or tabouli type dishes, etc. All work well in whole grain cereals and can be used in baked goods as well.

When wishing to sprout **oats**, choose only *hulless oats* (a variety that grows naturally without a hull) specified for sprouting. We recommend sprouting these for no more than a day to keep bitterness to a minimum. Most oats, including steel cut, rolled or flaked, oat groats (hulled oats), and common hulless oats are steamed to reduce rancidity and extend shelf life, thus producing un-sproutable oats. *Un-hulled* raw oats do sprout, but are meant for growing and not for use in foods as they have hulls too tough to chew. *You won't find sprouted oats in our recipes as we have found that funky tastes are common* *when we do. This is especially true when used in raw recipes where they are processed with any form of sweetener (a terrible soapy taste occurs) and/or when fermented (they become overly sour and odd).*

After sprouting, grains can be dehydrated at 110°-115° until dry for long term storage and/or used for flour, in cereals, etc.

Legumes—

The legume family is extensive and includes many varieties of beans, peas, lentils, soybeans, and peanuts. Some of the most nutritious and enjoyable, and therefore ones we tend to use most often, are **red, adzuki, mung** and **garbanzo beans, lentils,** and **peanuts.**

Raw dry legumes are required for sprouting, including peanuts. Some research indicates that garbanzo beans, lentils, mung beans, and sweet peas may be safe to consume as raw *sprouts* when eaten in moderation...if your system can handle them. Alfalfa sprouts, also a legume, are said to be safe in moderation as well, but only if sprouted to maturity (a minimum of 5 days). *All legumes are indigestible and toxic in varying degrees when eaten uncooked and un-sprouted. Thorough cooking ensures the safest and most agreeable form of digestion and assimilation. It is for this reason that all recipes in this book which contain legumes call for them to be cooked.*

Red beans are harder to track down than many other varieties but because of there attributes of delicious taste and nutritional superiority are worth the effort (see "Resources"). **Adzuki** or **aduki beans** have relatively bland flavor but are highly nutritious and work well where a neutral flavored legume is desired. Perhaps the most widely used and consumed legumes in the world are **lentils** and **garbanzo beans**, from flour in baked goods to hummus and dhal, these guys perform. **Mung bean** sprouts can grow to 1" or more very rapidly simply in a jar and are one of the most nutritious legumes. Great in stir fries, soups, our *dosas*, etc.

Peanuts have gotten a bad rap because of their potential to contain *aflatoxin* (a carcinogen), pesticide contamination, and rancid fats (from high temperature roasting), but when fresh organic peanuts are sprouted and cooked at low temperatures (as described in our *Peanut Butter* recipe) these concerns can be virtually eliminated. *When boiled, peanuts retain 10 times more of the anti-oxidant "resveratrol" than when roasted.*

Chapter 6

Fermenting

Before the invention of refrigeration, fermentation had been highly utilized around the globe to provide preservation, protection and nourishment. Grains, meats, dairy, roots, tubers and greens were all able to be stored for extended periods while porridges, breads, condiments and beverages could be kept on hand safely. It was even discovered that fermentation had the ability to transform toxins and inedible food sources into valuable nourishing sustenance, increasing both the variety and nutrients found in the often limited food supply of early peoples.

With the help of fermentation foods became more available, beneficial, and nourishing, with many having miraculous health and therapeutic value. You may have heard of some of these living legends, **kimchi** with its origins in Korea is a daily condiment enjoyed for its tasty digestive, cardio, cholesterol lowering, anti-cancer, and liver enhancing benefits. **Beet kvass** from the Ukraine is well documented as a tonic for the liver, gallbladder and kidneys. Its attributes include superior hydration, blood alkalization and oxygen carrying ability, high amounts of nourishing B vitamins, minerals and probiotics. The infamous **sauerkraut** from Germany is an activist for digestion, is anti-cancer, has antioxidants, vitamin U that benefits the healing of peptic ulcers, a great source of vitamin K necessary for the building of strong bones, and of course its claim to fame, high amounts of vitamin C (saving many a sailor on long voyages at sea). **Kefir**, which as far as we know came into being over 2000 years ago in the Caucasus Mountains as a method for preserving milk, is a highly beneficial fermented food/beverage that is typically made from dairy.

Water kefir, a dairy free version that we use in this book, is a refreshing, easy to make, slightly fizzy, tangy, lightly sweet drink with numerous health benefits, including the prevention and treatment of tuberculosis, ulcers, diarrhea, colitis, reflux, colon and prostate cancers along with all the other digestive system benefits that trillions of helpful micro organisms provide.

Making water kefir requires the use of water kefir grains (these are different from the grains to culture milk kefir), which are not grains at all but actually small clusters of bacteria, yeast, and polysaccharides. Kefir grains are sometimes available in health food stores but can also be found online. Buying *live* kefir grains is well worth the effort as freeze dried grains and powders take a much longer period to become active and/or can only be used to make one or two batches of inferior kefir. Directions for making kefir can be found in *"Beverages"*.

Water Kefir grains and the tasty beverage they make.
An internet search for "Dom's Kefir Insite" will get you to a site where you can learn all about kefir, including its many uses.

Due to inconsistency fermented foods are very difficult to produce commercially, therefore many of the fermented foods found on supermarkets shelves such as pickles, sauerkraut, olives, etc. are simply foods that have been packed in salt and/or vinegar, pasteurized, and are void of any beneficial properties whatsoever. Quality fermented foods are however becoming more available in quality supermarkets and health food stores. To be sure you are getting *live* beneficial fermented foods make sure it is stated on the label. Most live vegetable ferments such as sauerkraut, kimchi and pickles will only be found in the refrigerated section and will typically have an expiration date of about 3 to 6 months. *We will be showing you just how easy these foods are to create at home!*

Direct and indirect benefits that these and other pro-life foods create are almost endless and of tremendous value to our inner eco-system and state of health. Today many of us are re-discovering our roots and the simple yet profound health enhancing benefits that fermentation has been providing for centuries, some of which include:
- Increased enzymes which perform many vital tasks, including transforming proteins and carbohydrates into highly usable forms of readily assimilated nutrients.
- Benefit to the immune system, 85% of which is located in the gut!
- Superior forms and levels of probiotics than those found in probiotic supplements.

- Improvement and treatment of mood and mental health disorders including Alzheimer's and dementia.
- Reduced glucose levels in fermented foods which produce a more balanced and diabetic friendly food.
- Prevention and treatment of obesity through increased metabolism, digestion, assimilation, and more.
- Increased B vitamins and the creation of others, including B-12.
- Boosted levels of vitamin C and omega 3 fatty acids.
- The creation of amino acids such as *lysine* (absent from many of our foods) and *metheonine,* thus creating a more *complete protein*.
- The elimination of binding and inhibiting agents like phytic acid, oxalic acid, tannins, lectins and other anti-nutrients. *This elimination frees up a tremendous amount of energy, minerals, and nutrients enabling digestion and all other systems to operate with greater efficiency and ease while providing quality nourishment and energy...as opposed to depletion and degeneration produced from poorly digested foods and their anti-nutrients.*
- The production of antibiotic and anti-carcinogenic substances which disable harmful bacteria, yeasts, viruses, and other foreign invaders.
- Some of the best chelators for drawing out a variety of toxins and heavy metals.
- The prevention, protection, and cure from and for the many dangerous pathogens and harmful substances that we are under attack from in our ever changing everyday environment.

Ferments have become some of our favorite foods. We have come to truly enjoy and appreciate creating and consuming these *pro-life* foods and find ourselves and our kitchen in a constant process of creation...these foods *will grow* on you! If you're not familiar with the process or the many delicious foods fermenting can create, you will discover a fun, easy and rewarding method that fulfills an essential purpose and craving within. In fact for many, the most difficult part of the fermentation process is simply getting used to the idea of eating food that is teaming with life and transformed by living organisms!

We use the process of lactic acid fermentation, which is an anaerobic (sealed jar) process in where naturally occurring lactobacilli in the food create lactic acid that in turn preserves, protects, and transforms them. *Bad bacteria cannot live in this environment.*

The only requirement is jars, lids, a little planning, and then time to reap the incredible benefits of these larger than life microscopic well-beings to work their magic!

Here are things to keep in mind for successful fermentation:
- Foods being fermented in a liquid medium must be kept submerged to prevent mold and encourage lactic acid production.
- All equipment used, such as jars, lids, spoons, etc. need to be cleaned thoroughly so as to not introduce foreign types of bacteria.
- Moderate temperatures are best, 60 - 80 degrees is optimal.
- Most vegetables can be fermented with only the addition of salt,

simply chop vegetables and cover with a brine solution of 1-3 tablespoons of quality salt to 1 quart water.
- For a low sodium method, use other forms of fermenting agents such as 1-2 tablespoons rejuvelac, apple cider vinegar, or the liquid of a previously fermented batch, per quart. *Ferment starters such as these will also speed up the process.* The addition of a small amount of salt even to these ferments can improve flavor and help to keep veggies crisp as well as with preservation.
- Different fermenting agents will create different and unique tastes, try various ones to see which appeal to you as well as for creating the tastes you desire!
- Experiment, cut vegetables in a variety of sizes and shapes for different tastes and textures.

We hope you are both excited and inspired to get those jars a brewin! Once you discover how easy and deliciously different these foods are you will be enjoying the rewards of these functional foods, as they are often called, for the numerous functions they provide. It's no wonder many peoples still rely on fermented foods in their daily lives for their protection, preservation, and the numerous health benefits they bestow. By offering these foods regularly you will give new health, variety, taste, protection, and nourishment to your being.

Chapter 7

Vices Made Nicer

Chances are every one of us is *well* aware of a food...or two (or three!) that persists in our diet which should not be allowed access to the sacred temple, but for reasons of simple likes, wants, habits, or addictions, are allowed admittance anyway. Even the best intentioned of us can falter at the alter of desire! In this section we'll offer up some tips, tricks, alternatives, and options to make some of those enemy vices play nicer.

Tips #1, before indulging try to remember that yes, we are what we eat, but more importantly we become what we accumulate!

The Sacred Cup

Of course we're referring to coffee...even though sacred may be an understatement for some! Thanks to its stimulating, comforting, pleasing rich taste and addictive qualities, coffee is the most beloved substance available outside the black market. Worship to this black bean is a religion of its own with a very large group of loyal followers...many of whom would rather fight than face a day without their savior the "Gosh O' Mighty Joe"!

Coffee is one of those controversial consumables that can be touted as either divine or deadly, depending on what and whose information you choose. *The more we covet the more selective our hearing becomes.* Something to keep in mind when evaluating a food or beverage for consumption, *and yes you should be evaluating,* is that the facts about that substance may have been tweaked a bit...and even a bit more depending upon motives and who's doing the study. *Is the research that deems its benefits and harms based on analysis of freshly picked organically grown beans which are still raw, unrefined and unprocessed, or based on analysis of beans that have been fermented, chemically processed, refined and roasted.*

Out of the 350 plus chemicals naturally contained in coffee beans, some of these substances are actually beneficial, but unfortunately coffee has a dark side. All in all when you get to the bottom of the cup the destructive behaviors of coffee far exceed its benefits.

The dark side is that coffee has an extremely acidic effect upon the body creating depletion and weakness throughout the system. *Acidity is exacerbated in coffee beans when their natural oils turn rancid...this occur very quickly (usually within 2 weeks of roasting).* Along with this is the beating taken by the already over worked adrenals and nervous system. Add to this the fact that coffee consumption is comparable to biological warfare, every cup works at eliminating our ARMY of billions of micro super heroes known as good bacteria or micro flora. These warriors for health protect us from all kinds of foreign invaders, viruses, bacteria and pathogens while converting and creating nutrients, antioxidants and enzymes as well as performing many other life giving and sustaining activities.

So...you say you still demand the right to bear the brew??... Okay...although it won't win the war, here are some ways to help cut down enemy forces...until you're ready for internal peace anyway!

- Start with "organic" coffee beans or beans from sources that do not use chemical pesticides, as most "conventional" beans come from heavily sprayed plants.
- Select light roast beans. The darker the roast the more oils are pushed from within beans to the surface where they rancid much more quickly.
- After 2 weeks of roasting beans rancid quickly, so brew from freshly roasted beans.
- Cold brew coffee to greatly reduce its acidifying effects. *Check out our "Cold-Brewed Coffee" recipe, along with other divine ways to fly through your day, in "Beverages".*

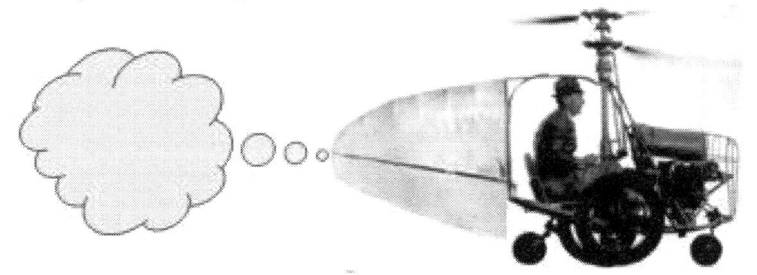

Ingredients for Good

Believe it or not even baked goods can be created to supply nutritional benefit above and beyond the simple mind numbing enjoyment they're known for. Our recipes do this without thought, but for creative types the following information can help in crafting your own gratifying goods:

- *Use organic whole food ingredients whenever possible.* Foods produced naturally, without the use of synthetic compounds or alterations to their design, are kinder to us and our environment.

- *Use whole grains and process just before use.* Most commercial ready to go pre-packaged flours consist of grains with their germ and bran removed to extend shelf life. This practice of castrating and skinning grains strips them of vital oils and fiber content, leaving only lifeless starchy skeleton of a once vital grain. To make matters worse, the nutritional value of grains (including whole grains) greatly and rapidly diminishes following their refinement into flour. What this means is *any* flour sitting in bins or packages on *any* shelf is equivalent to high glycemic nutrient void specs of dust with greater potential to cause harm than good.

    Along with using whole grains, prepare only the amount of flour needed for a recipe. *If you do have extra, place in an airtight container, refrigerate and try to use within a few days.* Grinding grain is quick and easy but does require a grain grinder or capable blender. Whole grains will make moister flour with a nuttier fresher taste. Whole un-processed grains will remain fresh and viable for a year or more when kept in a cool dry place. *Adding a few bay leaves repels bugs if they are a problem.*

- *Sprout & dehydrate whole grains to optimize nutrition.* Grains get a big boost in nutrition when allowed to germinate. When sprouted and dehydrated grains will keep for up to 3 months, allowing this most beneficial form of grain to be kept on hand and available for immediate use.

- *Use a healthier sweet in your treat.* Since whole foods are always best, naturally sweet ones like **apples, bananas, pineapple, dates** and **prunes** can all contribute to the sweetening and lessening of other concentrated sweeteners in recipes. They also offer varying degrees of moistness and flavor that can benefit many dishes. If additional moistness is not desired, cut back on any liquid ingredients and/or when baking, lower temperature 25° and cook a little longer.

    Succanat or **Rapadura** (same thing different name) is un-refined dried cane sugar and as such adds a nice molasses flavor. One of the best non-raw sugars and likely the least altering to a recipe when using to replace other dry granular sugars.

    Date sugar is dates dried and ground into a granular form, and though a bit more gritty, is a convenient and whole food way to replace white or brown sugar. Use at an exchange of 2/3 c date sugar per 1 c white or brown sugar. *To make your own date sugar, seed and chop dates, bake at lowest oven temperature setting (usually 250°) until dry, blend into powder.*

    Coconut sugar or **crystals** are produced from the sap of cut flower buds of the coconut palm, and although available in liquid form, it's usually found and used as a granular sweetener. By volume it is less sweet than most other granular sugars and imparts a mild coco-nutty flavor.

For a liquid sweetener, **date syrup** (see recipe), grade B *real* **maple syrup,** and *good* quality **agave nectar** are all good choices. *While a good choice to sweeten raw foods h*o*ney should not be used for cooking as it should never be heated above 104°.*

Besides using a healthier sweetener, pick on recipes that call for less, and/or reduce the amounts in ones that do. *Most of our recipes have already taken this into consideration!*

- **When cooking use quality oils that can take the heat.** It is now well recognized that hydrogenated oils from highly refined polyunsaturated vegetable oils in products like margarine and shortening are extremely harmful. Even the purported "healthy" ones aren't far behind when heated above their "smoke point" (capacity to handle heat before toxins and denaturing set in). **Unrefined coconut oil** and **canola oil** have a high smoke point and therefore are recommended for baking. *Canola oil must be organic since conventional is known to contain toxic contaminants from growing and extraction processes.* **Palm** and **palm kernel oil** have similar traits to coconut oil but are linked to deforestation and global warming so are not supported or recommended.

- *Avoid baking powder and baking soda.* While these are typically the leavening agents of choice, they deplete baked goods of their B vitamins and minerals, and because of a type of alkalinity they create in our body, deplete us of vitamin C. When sodium bicarbonate (baking soda) is absorbed into the blood stream it has been shown to decrease the flow and supply of oxygen in the body. For a healthier more natural leavening agent use ferments like **sour dough starter**, **amasake**, or **rejuvelac** which allow both our food and us to digest and utilize more effectively and beneficially.

- *Go Vegan.* Substitutions can easily be made to keep recipes vegan.
  - Replace *dairy milk* or *cream* with **nut** or **seed milks**.
  - Replace *butter* with **coconut oil**. Equal amounts of **apple sauce** or **puréed prunes** can also be added to oil.
  - Replace *eggs* with 1 T of ground **flaxseed** in 3 T of water for each egg replaced and let stand for 10 minutes.

Chocolate

Like coffee, chocolate has its die hard followers as well as research that either justifies or condemns its use. Thanks to fat, sugar, caffeine, theobromine (a caffeine like substance), and probably a few more of the 300+ substances found in chocolate, it provides a seemingly heavenly experience. The reality however points to chocolate as a bit of ahh...devilish delight!

While much research and plenty of personal experience indicates that positive aspects of chocolate do exist, when we look at the bigger picture and take into account the whole of its character, chocolate does appear to be worthy of its place in the vice department.

For some, varying degrees of negative effects occur when consuming even small amounts of chocolate, others may not be aware of its effects until larger amounts are consumed. Many of these negative effects may be attributed to the high amounts of oxalic acid, an anti-nutrient that binds up minerals and can create havoc on an already acidic system, and/or the caffeine and theobromine which effect neurotransmitter and central nervous system activity, which can include symptoms such as fatigue, insomnia, depression, anxiety, high blood pressure, headaches, PMS, paranoia, etc...

So...if paranoia hasn't set in yet and you still want your coco, let's see what we can do...

Sorry...after looking at the mounting evidence, as well as being honest about our own personal experiences with chocolate, we must recommend abstinence...and are still working on it!

...well, since that didn't work, the next obvious recommendation is to cut back consumption as much as possible. We can Zen and take a really long time thoroughly enjoying a really small amounts of chocolate, or we can make our own modified version. Carob with its chocolate *like* properties is said to be a good substitute for chocolate...though they must mean on some other planet! We have found however, by using chocolate and carob together the taste of chocolate can actually be enhanced. Besides nutritional superiority over chocolate, carob is sweeter, creating less need for sugars in recipes. The taste of carob varies from raw to roasted and from brand to brand, so if you don't care for the one you chose, try another. *Because carob is a legume it should not be eaten raw. Most carob labeled "raw" has received a little roasting to remedy the issue, so is ok, just don't seek out "truly raw" carob powder. At the other extreme, avoid carob that has been excessively roasted (dark and burnt tasting).*

Another step toward healthier chocolate may be to utilize raw unprocessed cacao. Homemade chocolate using cacao is very easy and rewarding to make...just try not to reward yourself too much! Some may experience cacao to be more stimulating than the processed variety, as it will generally contain higher amounts of many properties due to its lack of processing. This along with its richer flavor seems to offer satisfaction while consuming less. If you experience anxiety or other negative effects you may have consumed too much, or cacao may just not be right for you. The draw backs of processed chocolate include, long hours of oxidization, tempering, and various levels of heating and other refinement processes which diminish those healthful elements that chocolate contains. All and all we feel unprocessed cacao is a wiser choice and have chosen it for our recipes.

By the way... at a class on longevity I attended, the researcher stated that out of the 100 robust subjects aged 80-100 who were interviewed, there were two common denominators: 1) Almost all were vegetarians, and 2) They ALL ate chocolate!

Popcorn

This classic favorite has made its way to the vice department solely based on the company it keeps. When properly prepared however, popcorn can be a fairly healthy choice for satisfying the craving that only it can fulfill!

As far as cooking, air popping (air popping machine required) is healthiest as there is no need for oil. The next best is to use **coconut oil**. Using a wok with a lid on high heat works great for cooking popcorn. The small diameter wok bottom requires less oil and helps keep popcorn out of oil after popping. Also, the placing of paper towels under the lid, and secured by lid, absorbs excess oil as kernels pop. Turn off heat as soon as popping subsides.

After popping, a drizzle of **flaxseed oil** and/or **olive oil** will enhance the popcorn experience. *While oil is not necessary, it does allow salt and other spices to stick much better than without.* To add nutrition as well as a real honest to goodness buttery flavor, stir **nutritional yeast** into oil first, or sprinkle on after. For additional flavor and variety, sprinkle on spices of choice. *Use organic spices to ensure they have not been irradiated.* For salt, always use **unrefined sea salt,** instead of harmfully heated and minerally deprived refined "table salt".

Ice Cream

Yes, we all SCREAM for ice cream! But to keep screaming into old age, modification to the typically offered cold and creamy treat is required. Most ice cream, including ice cream alternatives, are loaded with poor quality fats, refined sugars, and a list of other poor quality ingredients and chemicals. The best option for health and for real satisfaction is to use real food...we offer several options in "Desserts"..so simple, so good, it will keep you screaming well into old age!

Chapter 8

Tips & Tidbits

This chapter is comparable to that junk drawer you have at home...it's all worthless!...that is until you need it or consciously decide to put some of its contents to good use!

Whether you find this content helpful, insightful, or simply entertaining, we do hope that it assists in some way to create more health and joy in your life.

Real Salt—

"Real Salt" is both the name of a salt produced by Redmond Products and a statement referring to the type of salt that should be used, a whole natural sea salt that has not been heated, processed, bleached, or chemically altered.

Most salts available from supermarkets or sitting on restaurant table tops are highly refined, chemically altered (to 99.5%+ sodium chloride) and stripped of nearly all sixty of their trace minerals. Anti-caking chemicals are added to keep refined salts from absorbing moisture while in a container, but this also means it won't be absorbed after it enters our body either. Potassium iodine as well as sugar (dextrose) to stabilize the iodine are used as well. Ironically, bleach is also used to make salt appear pure. Refined salts are subjected to high levels of heat in the process of drying them, which changes it's chemical structure to one that causes and contributes too many negative effects when introduced to the body.

It is the consumption of refined and processed salt that has lead to ill health and given salt a bad rap. Real salt (whole un-adulterated salt) is a safe and beneficial condiment when used in moderation (individual needs will vary). The mineral profile of real salt is similar to that of our blood, it has alkalizing and purification qualities, strengthens digestion, counteracts toxins in the body, neutralizes the effects of impure food or poor food combining, and more.

Himalayan Salt is an ancient pure salt void of environmental pollutants and full of trace minerals and other beneficial elements which make it healthful to use as well. *Himalayan salt has more potent salty flavor than other salts so far less may be needed.*

Check Stems for Freshness—

When selecting cherries or grapes look beyond the fruit for bright green flexible stems, if their brown, brittle or withering, the fruit is old.

Simply Good Canning Method—

A sugar free no hassle method of canning/preserving fruit. *The method of choice used for generations...generations ago!*

Use fruit that's ripe but not overly ripe.
Use wide mouth jars with domed lids.

Steps to canning:

- Wash jars and lids in hot soapy water and dry well.
- Thoroughly wash and optionally peel, remove seeds, pits, stems, etc.
- Fill jars to within ½" from top with fruit and secure lids.
- Place jars of fruit in a large pot or kettle.
- Place rags, straw, etc. between jars (prevents rattling during boiling).
- Fill pot or kettle with water to necks of jars.
- Bring to a boil and boil for 30 minutes.
- Turn off heat and let sit for 20 minutes before removing jars to cool.
- After 24 hours of cooling check to see if lids have sealed properly by removing bands and pressing the middle of the lids with a finger. If lid pops up when released, lid is not sealed properly, either process again as instructed above, refrigerate and use within 3 weeks, or transfer to a plastic container or baggie and freeze.
- Store in a dark cool place.

After opening fruit should be refrigerated and used within 3 weeks.

Sugar Patrol—

Cinnamon, clove, turmeric, and bay leaves all stimulate insulin activity to help the body process and control sugars more efficiently. Cinnamon is the most powerful...as well as happens to be complimentary to many sweets.

Root Relief—

Ginger and turmeric, whether fresh or in powder form, have been found to significantly and consistently provide relief from pain, inflammation and stiffness (such as that caused by rheumatoid arthritis).

Live Long & Large!—

Researchers, scientists, health enthusiasts and laymen alike have long searched for secrets to long and healthy living. After analysis of all accumulation evidence, including study after study on real live old people, a true fountain of youth has been discovered! The secret...EAT LESS!

The common denominator between peoples studied who displayed the greatest vitality, energy, and rates of longevity, wasn't whether they were vegan or meat eater, rich or poor, lived in the tropics or the arctic; it was that they ate less food than most.

First to Go—

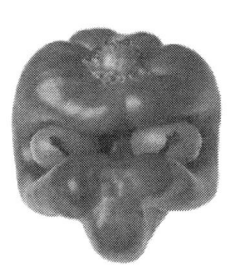

Even after fresh fruits and vegetables are picked they continue to breathe (absorb oxygen and release carbon dioxide), but in doing so they are using up their stores of natural sugars and antioxidants, so as time goes by they become less flavorful, more acidic, and contain fewer antioxidants. Some fruits and vegetables go through this process of deterioration faster than others and should be eaten shortly after harvest or before others that they came home with.

These include artichokes, arugula, asparagus, broccoli, brussel sprouts, cherries, corn, kale, lettuce, mushrooms, okra, parsley, raspberries, scallions, snap beans, spinach, and strawberries.

Keep the Crunch Captain—

When cooking asparagus, broccoli, brussel sprouts and cabbage, cook no longer than five minutes to avoid nutrient loss and retain natural flavor, sweetness, and crunch appeal. Cooking longer will cause sulfurous fumes to develop and compromise taste.

Onion 411—

To keep nutrients but lose the heat of strong pungent onions, cook, but not more than 5 min. or nutrients will be lost. Sweeter varieties typically only have about one third the antioxidants as stronger flavored varieties, but may be more suitable for salads and raw dishes. Oval or round red onions are typically hot while the flatter wider ones are mild and sweet. Yellow or white onions can be hot or sweet but hard to tell apart, rely on labels!

Purge your Pungents:

Chopping, slicing, dicing, etc. releases compounds contained in garlic, onions, and others in the alliums family, and waiting for at least ten minutes after doing so and before consumption, allows those compounds to reach full beneficial potential.

Reduce gas—

- To enhance overall intestinal health and digestion, thus reducing gas, include **fermented foods** in the diet on a regular basis. *Try starting meals with small amounts of sauerkraut, kimchi, or other ferment.*
- **Avoid coffee** which destroys beneficial flora and de-mineralizes and acidifies the digestive system.
- Add **lime juice** to reduce or eliminate the gaseous effects of carrot juice.
- Add sea weed like **Kombu** or **Wakame** when cooking beans. *Sprouting and fermenting beans are also highly effective.*
- **Ginger** in tea, hot water, or food can help with an upset stomach and calm down the digestive system.
- Eating or adding **peppermint** leaves or **raw honey** can help with the digestion of foods.
- When consuming fatty foods like desserts, **cinnamon** can help break down fats and eliminate gas caused by undigested food.
- **Fennel** after a meal can help with inflammation and combustion.
- **Flax seed** prevents gas as well as treats constipation.
- For better digestion avoid drinking water during or close to a meal, especially ice water, as it dilutes digestive juices. *Sip on small amounts of warm water with meals if necessary.*

Sugar Fix...QUICK!—

A nice fix we've discovered when craving sweets is to simply drink a small glass of date sweetened almond milk (see recipe). The mix of creamy and sweet always seems to do the trick...and quite a bit healthier than say...shooting a line of Oreos!

All about Coconuts—

      Coconuts and the many products derived from them are versatile ingredients that can enhance taste, texture, and nutrition in a wide range and variety of recipes. The types of whole coconuts available in non-tropical locations consist of either **brown** or **white husk coconuts**, found naked and hairy on store shelves, or **young Thai coconuts**, found with inner white husk or "coir" still intact, plastic wrapped, and refrigerated.

      White and brown husk coconuts are mature coconuts. The meat of white husk coconuts is easier to remove, more flexible, and contains less fat than that of the brown husk coconuts. The meat of either is ideal for making coconut milk, coconut butter, and shredded coconut.

      Young Thai coconuts are easier to open, have sweeter and softer meat that is easier to remove, and contain more water than husk coconuts. These attributes make them the coconut of choice for many dishes, especially desserts and beverages.

Choosing a coconut: When choosing coconuts simply shake and choose ones with the most water/weight to ensure both freshness and unbroken shells.

Getting into a husk coconut - First remove the water by either piercing two of the eyes with an ice pick or phillips head screwdriver. A drill with a clean 3/8" drill bit works well also. Pour water into a receptacle. Crack shell by holding coconut in one hand and a large heavy cleaver in the other then striking the center of the coconut again and again around its circumference with the *blunt* side of the clever until it splits or separates enough to pull apart with your hands. Another option is to hold the coconut on a solid surface like a large rock and hit it with a hammer or another rock around its circumference with just enough force and repetitions to create a continuous crack.

      The best way to get the thick meat out of the shell is with a coconut *demeating tool* (found at some Oriental markets or on line), otherwise use a sturdy knife and repetitiously push the blade as far down as possible between meat and shell prying meat out as you go. *Besides easier demeating a demeating tool gets meat out in bigger pieces making them easier to hold for grating, shredding, etc.*

Getting into a Young Thai Coconut - It may take a little practice, but young Thai coconuts are fairly easy to get into. We prefer a method that we call the *carve & tap method*. Starting with a serrated knife, carve off the white fibrous husk at the top of the coconut until you can see a 3-4" diameter area of hard shell. *This exposes the "sweet spot", an area that is easiest to break into!* Then with the back/blunt side of a butcher type knife and a snap of your wrist, tap around the exposed shell until a crack begin to form (around the "sweet spot"). Insert tip of knife into crack and pry off the top.

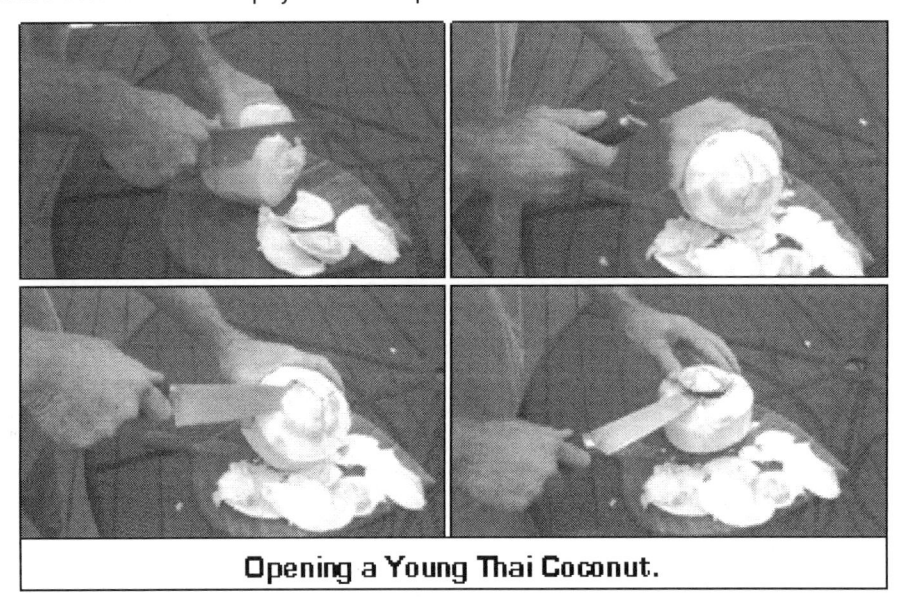

Opening a Young Thai Coconut.

When pouring out coconut water, tip quickly and pour into a wide mouth container to avoid loss. The meat from a young Thai coconut can range anywhere from a soft gel to a thick rubber like substance. In most cases it will come out fairly easily using a large spoon. Start from the top and scrape the inside surface in a circular spiral fashion toward the bottom and remove meat.

Coconut products: There are an ever increasing number of products derived from coconuts showing up in virtually every kind of market place. There's coconut oil, butter, amino acids, vinegar, nectar, crystals, flour, and others. These products can provide some of the same health benefits as whole coconuts as long as the steps that were taken to create them have not altered or destroyed natures original work. When choosing these products try to acquire from reputable sources or manufactures and ones that display statements such as "raw", "un-refined", "un-bleached", etc. on their labels.

See more about the coconut products we use in our recipes by viewing "Ingredient Definitions" at the end of "Recipe" chapter.

The Big Picture

Through the process of our life's work we have been continuously reminded of the fact that no matter how worthy the knowledge or diligent the effort is pursued to generate and maintain wellness, life and its health can be no greater than that which supports it. Its source cannot be isolated or manufactured, and our ability to be well in body requires the wellness of all that supports it.

It is all about you!...You and Me that is...but how about everyone else? The bees and the trees, the whales and the worms, the soil and the sheep, and all the other incredible forms that life takes. Evolution and progress seems to have taken us by the nose and down a path that has far removed us from our source and resources.

In the acknowledgment of our superior intelligence, we as humans have isolated and defined our importance and existence over that of all other forms of life and creation. Our precarious identity and self-centered actions have severely tipped the scales of balance. We can observe our destruction both environmentally and scientifically through the depletion, poisoning, and alteration of the Earths ecosystem and resources. And what we seemingly fail to recognize, or choose to ignore, is that we are creating the same destruction, poisoning, and depletion in our own health and state of being.

It is about us...You and Me...as humans *we* are the only beings capable and responsible for the conscious choosing of our own fate as well as the fate of all other life forms on this planet. Through supply and demand we fuel our economic system along with its decisions and developments that have such a tremendous impact on our environment and future. In our everyday choices we hold the power and the voice for change. The choice to support sustainable, non GMO, environmentally friendly and humane practices and products is a pledge that supports the existence and future for all!

Within the intention of this book is the hope for wellness...for that of our being and of our source. We urge you to become informed of the condition and situation of the planet and its many expressions of life, as well as to live in awareness of the contents and effects that your choices contribute to everyday.

Chapter 9

Food Preparation

Pick from tree, vine, bush or ground and put into mouth...simple! But no...somewhere along the way we evolved into a complacent yet sophisticated bunch that now needs an arsenal of skills and tools in order to achieve the once simple task of consuming foods that both sustains and satisfies us. Throughout this book we have worked to keep both foods and methods simple, but still, before plunging into the recipes it may prove fruitful to check out some information on Kitchen Equipment, Chef Basics, and Recommended Foods to Have on Hand for additional insight into creating these healthy satisfying recipes as easily and conveniently as possible.

Kitchen Equipment

While we are not experts or even particularly knowledgeable about all of the various types and brands of equipment available, we have made it around the butcher a few times and feel we do have some experience to share. What follows is a look at some equipment and other food preparing paraphernalia that we have found useful to our ways along with other information that we thought might be of value.

High speed blender - Thanks to its versatility and ease of use, a quality high speed blender is the most useful and important piece of equipment in the kitchen. From making soups (including the heat) to nut butters and flours, these blenders open the doors to creating a plethora of healthful foods with ease.

Vita-mix was one of the first publicly available quality blenders.

Today however, they do have a few worthy competitors. We've had a Vita-mix for 15+ years now and have used it virtually every day 2-3 times a day...on show days hundreds of times! Besides recently replacing the blades it's been maintenance free and works great, because of this we have not gotten to try any other brands, but have heard good to mixed reviews about others out there. *We have never heard anyone express sorrow about buying this high quality blender...even considering the $375+ price tag!*

Food Processor - Comes in handy for quantity chopping, mixing, and the making of "*I Scream*". There are many to choose from and can be acquired anywhere from your local department store to your local thrift shop. Small food processors come in handy for smaller amounts (i.e. handful of herbs or nuts, etc.)...which often times larger versions are incapable of.

Champion juicer - This brand name and one of a kind juicer is rare among juicers in that it masticates what your juicing instead of chopping or shredding at high speed with centrifugal force, creating less chance for oxidization and therefore nutrient loss. Along with making nut and seed butters out of whole nuts and seeds, the mastication method allows other whole foods to be processed with a texture that would be difficult to create in any other way.

Dehydrator - More than just a method of preserving food, dehydrating can produce a supply of ready to go grains (after sprouting) as well as tasty crunchy snacks made from veggies, nuts, seeds, and others. While drying can be performed in an oven, most do not allow temperatures low enough (below 115°) to preserve heat sensitive nutrients and enzymes.

The "Excalibur" is a popular and reputable brand with several options and models to choose from. *We've had one for 30 years with no complaints.* Whichever brand or model you choose, be sure it is one that allows good airflow around all trays and is equipped with a thermostat (most are). *A timer might be a nice feature also, but not really necessary since dehydrating times are so variable as well as the fact that the test of doneness can only be verified through examination.* Our recommendation is to simply dehydrate foods at 110° until desired dryness is achieved.

Nut milk (plus) bag - Various mesh or cloth bags with draw strings called nut milk bags, produce bags, muslin bags, etc. are available and can be used universally to perform such tasks as covering sprouting jars if you run out of lids, draining cold brewed coffee, making cheese, and of course making nut milks. After trying out various materials and various mesh patterns, we settled on organic cotton canvas (non-mesh) bags (sold as produce bags). They are inexpensive and easier to work with than the heavier hemp bags and last much longer than mesh bags.

Citrus squeezer/juicer - A gadget that you can live without, but if you want to live without it, don't try it! There are different sizes for limes, lemons and oranges, and besides potentially saving your hand at a lemon aid party, they squeeze out every bit of juice as well as hold onto the seeds.

Mandolin - An invaluable tool if you do lots of slicing and dicing. *Dices an onion before tears ever get a chance!* Comes with different blades for different tasks and can usually be adjusted for thickness as well. We prefer our $30 model ("Borner") over our $150 dollar one.

Veggie noodle maker - Making noodles from vegetables such as zucchini and jicama opens up a whole new way for culinary expression and texture. There are a number of variously priced products, including the "Spiralizer", that will turn out veggie noodles of various sizes and shapes. We've been happy with our $40 Japanese model, the "Benriner Cook Helper Slicer".

Garlic press - Presses and minces at the same time to release garlic's nutrients and infamous flavor and odor. Can be a real time saver as cloves can even be pressed without peeling first. A garlic press can also be used for mincing and getting the juice out of other foods like hot peppers and ginger root as well. Just make sure you get a heavy duty model as many break easily. Self cleaning features are nice too.

Helping Hands - Don't forget about the best help of all while preparing nurturing foods in the kitchen, helping hands!

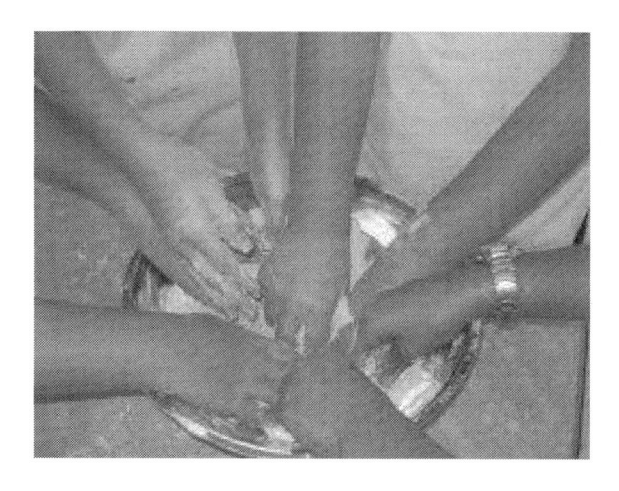

Chef Basics

The following are helpful guidelines to ensure recipes turn out as tasty and healthful as possible:

1) **Use high quality ingredients** - A recipe is only as good as its ingredients...in taste and nutrition, so go for quality! Besides buying from farmers markets for in season fresh fruits and vegetables, inquire to acquire fresh and viable nuts, seeds, grains and legumes from reputable sources committed to quality. The ultimate test to determine the quality of nuts, seeds, grains, and legumes is to smell, taste, sprout, and consume them. If they do not sprout and/or appeal to you, especially when consumed, try another source.

2) **Store for freshness** - Once we have our high quality ingredients we will want to store them properly so they will stay that way. A 40° fridge is a good place to store most vegetables and some fruits, but others like tomatoes, potatoes, onions, garlic, melons, apples, berries, and stone fruits like peaches, apricots and plums will lose flavor and even nutrients if refrigerated, so instead keep these at room temperature and preferably in a cool dark place. *Once cut however these foods should be refrigerated if not used up by days end.* For grains and legumes, store in airtight containers in a cool dark place. Nuts and seeds contain fats that rancid quickly so should be refrigerated in glass jars with tight fitting lids. *Buy nuts with shells still intact whenever possible to optimize freshness.*

3) **Peel and seed sensibly** - Yes, consuming whole foods is *usually* best, but *please* discard skins and seeds that are hard, bitter, astringent, or otherwise inedible. If any portion of a food doesn't taste good by itself (i.e. banana and avocado skins and citrus seeds) then trust your instincts, don't eat it and don't include it in recipes.

4) **Use pure water** - Clean pure water is required for vital living, this includes food preparation. The chemicals chlorine and fluoride have been well researched and proven to be dangerous, *especially* when consumed, but are added to tap water anyway. *Chlorinated water can kill seeds preventing them from sprouting as well as kill good bacteria needed in the process of fermenting. If water does not support these life forms...it probably doesn't support ours either.* Most natural supplies of water including rivers, streams, springs, under water aquifers, and even rain water now contain various doses of pollutants as well. Reverse-osmosis (RO), de-ionization,

distillation, and other purification systems are good choices and now widely available through vending or in-home systems. Research will be your best bet for determining which is right for you. If your tap water is free of fluoride, you live in a relatively pollution free area, it tastes ok, and you want to use it, then at least allow chlorine to dissipate before consumption by filling a glass picture with water and allowing to sit uncovered for at least 24 hrs.

5) **Follow instructions** - As you have read in previous chapters, the benefits provided through sprouting, fermenting, etc. are many, and though some recipes can be prepared without these extra steps, they are methods highly recommended for your greatest good! Cooking methods, times, and temperatures are other instructions that have been thoughtfully paired with each recipe in order to create the least harm and achieve greatest overall results.

6) **Don't follow instructions** - Also where appropriate, various choices for ingredients are offered, for example *maple syrup, agave, or honey* may be listed as an ingredient when a sweetener is needed. While these foods have been placed in descending order from the one we feel is the best choice for the recipe, or simply to make it vegan, a different choice (including your own) should be made if it better suits your specific diet, condition, desire, or even to simply accommodate what you have on hand. *As you work with our recipes you will find that our processes are very basic/universal, and soon you will find how easy it is to alter and create a limitless variety of your own artisan concoctions!*

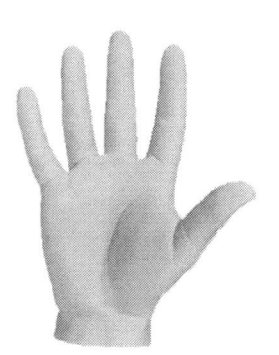

Foods to Have on Hand

Having the following food items on hand is totally optional, but will allow you to create a good many of the recipes found in this book quickly and easily: *List excludes produce.*

Non-prep food items:

The following are food items with a decent shelf life so can be acquired ahead of time. Whenever possible and applicable obtain these food items in their raw/live state. *See "Ingredient Definitions" for descriptor of food items.*

Pure (un-chlorinated) Water
Olive Oil (cold pressed unfiltered extra virgin).
Coconut Oil (preferably un-refined).
Spices - salt, pepper, cayenne pepper (whole and/or powdered), chili powder, onion and garlic granules or powder, cinnamon, and thyme.
Vanilla Powder or **Vanilla Beans.**
Dulse and/or **Kelp Flakes**
Miso (unpasteurized; soy or non-soy), and/or **Nama Shoyu**, and/or **Tamari** (wheat free is available).
Nutritional Yeast
Sweeteners - raw dates, agave and/or honey, maple syrup (pure grade B), sucanat and/or coconut sugar.
Dried Fruits - raisins, cherries, apricots, and/or other dried fruit.
Dried Shredded Coconut
Carob and/or **Cacao Powder**
Sun Dried Tomatoes (un-sulfured...which will be harder, but keep some soaking in water and in fridge to have readily available if used often).
Kalamata and/or other black (ripe) olives.
Nuts - almonds, cashews, walnuts (in shell), and/or other nuts.
Seeds - flax, chia, hulled sunflower, un-hulled sesame.
Grains - oats (flakes, steel cut, or groats) buckwheat (hulled), millet, whole kernel corn (dry), short grain brown rice, brown basmati and/or brown jasmine rice, and/or other grains.
Legumes - dried red beans, mung beans, adzuki beans, garbanzo beans, lentils, and peanuts (organic raw) and/or peanut butter (organic).
Soft Wheat (for making rejuvelac).

Prepared food items:

While a little preparation is required, once created the following food items supply readily available drinks, snacks, and ingredients. Many will last 1-3 weeks in the fridge. *See "Ingredient Definitions" for descriptor of food items.*
Water Kefir (p.64)
Almond Milk and/or other *Nut or Seed Milk* (p67)
Seed Cheese (p.132)
Dosas (p.113)
Tortillas (p.112)
Sauerkraut (p.145)
Mustard (p.144)
Nut Butter (p.131).

The following foods sprouted and dehydrated will keep for 3-6 months when properly stored:
Almonds (raw) for almond butter, almond milk, snacking, etc.
Buckwheat (raw hulled) **and other grains** for use in raw cereals, as flour in baking, etc,

Chapter 10

Recipes

    The recipes you are about to encounter contain ingredients for life! Created for celebrating the health, joy, and pleasure that occurs in the delicious and intimate relationship between you and that which nurtures you.

RECIPE KEY

Recipe Name

Here there may be a sentence or two describing the recipe and/or recommendations for use as well as other information.

Ingredients and amounts will be listed here.
Always feel free to substitute or change either of these based on what you have on hand or with what you feel may be a better choice for you.

Here you will find the directions meant to make the above ingredients come together in harmonious fashion. *Again, if not impressed change at will!*

* Additional suggestions or recommendations may be noted at the bottom of the recipe for an ingredient or ingredients listed above with a corresponding asterisk.

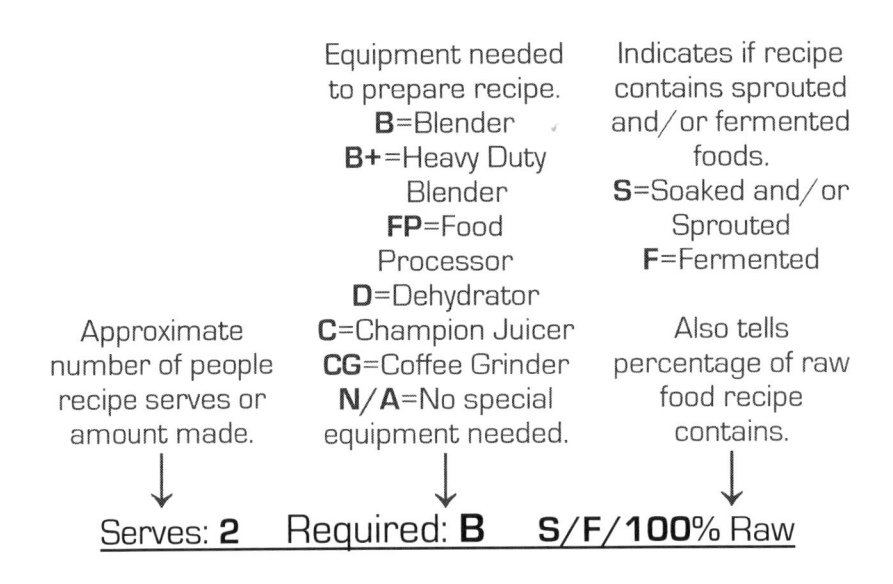

	Equipment needed to prepare recipe.	Indicates if recipe contains sprouted and/or fermented foods.
	B=Blender	
	B+=Heavy Duty Blender	**S**=Soaked and/or Sprouted
	FP=Food Processor	**F**=Fermented
	D=Dehydrator	
Approximate number of people recipe serves or amount made.	**C**=Champion Juicer	Also tells percentage of raw food recipe contains.
	CG=Coffee Grinder	
	N/A=No special equipment needed.	
↓	↓	↓

Serves: **2**   Required: **B**   **S/F/100**% Raw

RECIPE INDEX

Ingredient Definitions......166

Beverages & Bliss Blends
Water Kefir......64
Rejuvelac......64
Ginger Fizz......65
Liver Giver......65
Beet Kvass.....66
O.G. Carrot Kvass......66
Almond Milk.....67
Nut & Seed Milk......67
Coconut Milk......68
Paradise......68
Thai Chi Tea......69
Green Light......69

Beverages (Cold or Warm)
Cold Brewed Coffee......70
Matcha Latté.......70
Harmony Chai......71
Mayan Cacao......71

Bliss Blends
Seasonal Bliss......72
Pina Colada......72
Flying Gorilla.......73
Vanilla Date-Nut.....73
Brazilian Bliss......74
Nighty Night Bliss.....74

Breakfast Foods
Real cereal......76
Coconut Yogurt.......76
Fruit Seed Porridge......77
Macaw Mash......77
Papaya Boat.......78
Better Oats.....78
Millet-O-Meal......79
Coconut Cornmeal......79
Pancakes......80
Pumpkin Pancakes......80
Apple Spice Pancakes......81
Fiji Pancakes.......81
Sunrise Dosa......82

Snacks
Cauliflower Popcorn......84
Better Popcorn......84
Chickpea Fries......85
Onion Rings......85
Sesame Rice Crackers......86

Snacks (Dehydrated)
Crispy Crackers......86
Mineral Crunch Bars......87
Seasoned Almonds......87
Sweet & Spicy Walnuts......88
Chili-Lime Pistachios.....88
Green Seeds......89
Veggie Munch.....89
Apple Chewla......90
Hoola Chewla......90

Salads & Dressings
Plop Top Salad......92
Caesar Salad......92
Far East Coleslaw......93
Cool Hand Cuke......93
Whole Beet Salad.......94
Hot Head.......94
Confetti Salad.......95
Deviled Avos.......95

Salad Dressings
Raw Ranch......96
Date Dijon......96
Yeast Ahoy!......97
Sesame Ginger......97
Cilantro Avo.......98
Two Tomato Herb......98
Tahini Dressing......99
Creamy Kraut........99
Mustard Curry.......100
Herb Goddess.......100

Soups
Better Broth......102
Bloody Good Soup......102
Allium Soup......103
Tomato Curry......104
Pumpkin Chestnut......104
Hot Pot......105
Frijoles Soup......105
Legumenous Soup......106
Summer Squash......106
Broccauli Soup......107
Cauliflower Curry......107
African Peanut Stew......108

Main Meals
Main Meals (Accessories)
Seed Crusts......110
Veggie Seed Crusts......111
Chickpea Noodles......111
Tortillas......112
Chapati......112
Dosas......113
Fluffels......113

Main Meals
Fabulous 5......114
Sunshine Sandwich......114
Summer Delight......115
Mediterranean Boats......115
Portosteak Sandwich......116
Dhali Dolmas......116
Shitake Stir Fry......117
Quinoa Bowl......117
Dosa Pasties......118
Looky Like Sushi Roll......118
Squash Curry......119
Pumpkin Dosas......119
Falafels......120
Chickpea Lentil Burger......120
Garbanzo Krautdogs......121
Live Pizza......121
Garlic Dosa Pizza......122
Vegana Lasagna......122
Cauliflower Alfredo......123
Fettuzucchini-No-Afraido..123
Manicotti Raw......124
Dosa Manicotti......124
Zucchini Anti-Pasta......125
Spicy Beans & Rice......125
Chicks & Greens......126
Piñatas......126
Tostada......127
Enchiladas......127
Bandito Burrito......128
Sloppy Jose's......128

Sauces/Spreads/Dips
Oliveutter......130
Mayo......130
Nut & Seed Butters......131
Peanut Butter......131
Seed Cheese......132
Med Spread......132
Easy Cheesy......133
Sesame Caviar......133
Almond Satay......134
Sauercream......134
Hummus......135
Sunflower Hummus......135
Marinara Sauce......136
Spinach Walnut Pesto......136
Mushroom Marinade......137
Mushroom Sauce......137
Garlic Cream Sauce......138
Cashew Cream Sauce......138
Spicy Gringo Sauce......139
Enchilada Sauce......139
Bandito Dip......140
Salsamole......140
Mango Pico De Gallo......141
Apple Butter......141
Dried Fruit Butter......142
Hot Pepper Jam......142

Condiments
Mustard & Ketchup......144
Sauerkraut......145
Kimchi......145
Pickles......146
Pickled Veggies......146

Desserts
& Better Baked Goods
  Sprout Bread......148
  Lentil Bread......148
  Amasake......149
  Rice Pudding......149
  Chia Pudding......150
  All-Be-Good Bars......150
  Yin Yang Baklava......151
  Hazelnut Torte......151
  Sunflower Cookies......151
  Chocolate Chick Cookies......152
  Ginger Cookies......152
  Right Bites.......152
  German Cacao Brownies......153
  Beanie Brownies.......153
  Rocky Roll.......154
  Carob Fudge Crunch......154
  Raw Chocolate.......155
  Raw Chocolate NOW!......155
  Rio Good Bars......156
  Yum Yum Yams......156
  Carrot Pineapple Aspic......157
  Island Cakes.......157
  Pie Crust.......158
  Fruit Pie.......158
  Choc-O-Cherry Pie......159
  Butternut Pie.......159
  Cocopops.......160
  I Scream.......161
  Orange Sure-bet.......161

Desserts Toppings
Cacao Sauce.......162
Karma Sauce......162
Fruit Sauce......163
Date Syrup......163
Cashew Whip......164
Coconut Cream Whip......164
Raw Frosting/Icing.......165

Beverages & Bliss Blends

Water Kefir

For information on water kefir see "Fermenting" chapter.

6 c Pure Water
½ c Water Kefir Grains
½ c Sucanat
¼ tsp. Coral Calcium or sterilized and ground **Egg Shell.**

Place sucanat and calcium or egg shell in a ½ gallon jar, add enough warm water to dissolve sucanat, after dissolved add enough cool water to fill jar ¾ full, when mixture reaches room temperature add kefir grains, cover jar with an air tight lid and let sit to ferment for 24-48 hrs. *The longer mixture sits the more fermented/less sweet it will become, process within 3 days however, as kefir grains will begin to starve.* Process for use by pouring through a plastic or stainless steel strainer into a glass storage container, refrigerate liquid and repeat process with grains. *Grains multiply so simply remove some (keeping ½ c for next batch), either discard extra, use in smoothies, etc.*

Makes: **6 c**   Required: **N/A**   **F/100**% Raw

Rejuvelac

Fermented liquid providing friendly bacteria helpful in creating healthy intestinal flora. Drink as a refreshing beverage, use as a starter for fermentation, as a natural leavening agent in breads, or in dressings, sauces, etc.

2 c Soft Wheat, Rye, Spelt, Kamut, Barley, Millet*, Amaranth*, or Buckwheat* sprouted 2 days in half gallon jar.
Pure Water

Add water to sprouted grains leaving 1" of air space, cover with an air tight lid and allow to ferment at room temperature for 48 hours, strain finished rejuvelac liquid, use or store in fridge and use within 3-4 days. For a second and third batch repeat process with the same grains but ferment only 24 hours each time.
* Gluten free grains.

Makes: **½ G**   Required: **N/A**   **S/F/100**% Raw

Ginger Fizz

A lightly carbonated refreshing beverage that is oh so satisfying!

3 c *Water Kefir* (see recipe previous page).
1 tsp. Sucanat, Agave, or **Honey**
½ Lime juiced.
½ Lemon juiced.
1 T Fresh Grated Ginger

Combine ingredients into a jar with a tight fitting lid (allowing 1"+ air space), let stand at room temperature to ferment/carbonate for 24 hours, consume or store in fridge.

Serves: **2**   Required: **N/A**   **F/100**% Raw

Liver Giver

Give your hard working liver a hand with this cleansing and nourishing beverage. *Drink first thing in the morning or on an empty stomach for ultimate effect.*

3 c *Water Kefir* or ***Rejuvelac*** (see recipes previous page).
1 Apple cored and sliced.
2 tsp. Chlorella, Spirulina, or **½ tsp. Blue Green Algae** or a combo.
1-2" Fresh Ginger peeled.
4+ Kale Leaves of any variety.
½ Lemon or **lime** juiced.
1" Fresh Turmeric peeled or ½ tsp. powder.
1 Cayenne Pepper (fresh or dried, or pinch of powder; optional).

Blend all ingredients just until liquefied.

Serves: **2**   Required: **B**   **F/100**% Raw

Beet Kvass

This beautiful blood red tonic is good for...you guessed it...the blood, but also the bowels, liver, gut, etc. Use as a tonic as is, add to veggie drinks, salad dressings, etc.

3-4 Beets lightly scrubbed and diced.
1 T Real Salt or **½ T Himalayan Salt**
Pure Water as needed.

Place ingredients into ½ gallon jar, filling to within 1" from top with water, secure with an airtight lid, let sit at room temperature 5-7 days, refrigerate and strain as needed. *For next batch use 1 c of previous batch and ½ T salt in place of ferment starter.*

<u>Makes: **½ G**   Required: **N/A**   **F/100%** Raw</u>

O.G. Carrot Kvass

Orange and ginger flavored kvass...with effervescence if desired!

6 Carrots sliced.
2 T Fresh Ginger peeled and sliced or chopped.
1 Orange peel only cut into strips.
4 tsp. Real Salt
Pure Water as needed.

Place carrots, ginger and orange peel into a ½ gallon jar, add salt, fill rest of jar with water to 1" from top, cover with lid and shake to dissolve salt, let sit to ferment at room temperature 2-4 days (to desired sourness), strain liquid into a jar, store in fridge. *A second weaker batch can be made by leaving 1 c liquid in jar with carrot mixture, filling with water and fermenting as instructed above.*

To create effervescence: Place strained liquid kvass into an airtight jar with a pinch of sucanat or tsp. of maple syrup, agave, or honey, leave sit at room temperature for 3 days (to desired level of carbonation), store in fridge.

<u>Makes: **½ G**   Required: **N/A**   **F/100%** Raw</u>

BEVERAGES

Almond Milk

Creamylicious best describes this must have beverage and ingredient. Puts store bought to shame!...in both taste and nutrition.

1 c Raw Almonds soaked 12-18 hrs. then rinsed and drained.
3 c Pure Water
½ tsp. Vanilla Powder or ½ bean (optional).
3 Dates or sweetener of choice (optional).

Blend almonds and water well, strain through mesh or cloth bag into a large bowl, pour liquid back into blender, add vanilla and sweetener if desired, blend again. Store in fridge and use within 3-5 days (depends on quality of almonds).

For Almond Cream: Use 1 c less water.

Tip #1: Keep unsweetened almond milk on hand so that it can be used that way, then simply add desired amount of sweetener based on what you will be using it for.

Tip #2: When almond milk is called for in recipes like baked goods, pancakes, or others, straining out pulp may not be necessary.

Makes: **3+ c**   Required: **B**   S/**100**% Raw

Nut & Seed Milk

Some interesting and diverse milks can be made from the many nuts, seeds and grains available, here are some ideas and general guidelines...tweak to suite taste or need.

1 c Nuts like hazelnuts, walnuts, cashews, brazil nuts, etc. soaked 12-18 hrs. and thoroughly rinsed.
Or **1½ c Seeds** or **Cooked Grains** like hulled sunflower seeds, pumpkin seeds, amaranth, millet, etc. soaked 8-12 hrs., then thoroughly rinsed, drained, and cooked as directed.
3 c Pure Water

Thoroughly blend nuts, seeds, or grains with water, strain through a mesh or cloth bag into a large bowl, blend again with a sweetener if desired. Store in fridge in an air tight glass container.

Makes: **3+ c**   Required: **B**   S/**100**% Raw

BEVERAGES

Coconut Milk

Below are several techniques for making coconut milk from the two types of coconuts readily available.

Young Thai Coconut Milk: *Sweeter and softer flesh makes this a good milk for plain drinking, adding to smoothies, desserts, etc.*
Blend water & meat (1 coconut yields 2-3 cups milk).

Mature or Husk Coconut Milk: *Closer to canned version and more suitable for cooking.*
Blend water & meat of 1 coconut with 1c pure water, strain through a strainer pressing with a large spoon or through a cloth or mesh bag (1 coconut with added water yields 2-3 cups milk).

Easy Coconut Milk (from shredded coconut): *A simpler method of making a coconut milk suitable for cooking and other uses.*
2 c Shredded Coconut (raw unsweetened).
4 c Pure Water
Best if coconut is soaked in water for several hours, otherwise blend well and strain through a nut milk bag. *Left over pulp can be dried and used in recipes.*

Makes: **2-3 c**   Required: **B**   **100%** Raw

Paradise

Vanilla turns this one into a pretty exotic tasting drink, sure to impress everyone on your island!

1 ½ c Young Thai Coconut Water
½ Lime juiced.
¼ tsp. Vanilla Powder or ¼ bean.

Place all ingredients in a blender and blend for a moment...a moment longer if using vanilla bean instead of powder.

Serves: **1**   Required: **B**   **100%** Raw

Thai Chi

Creamy, coco-nutty, and delicious!

3 c Coconut Milk from either Young Thai or Husk coconuts (see opposing page for recipes).
1 c Prepared Tea Concentrate (1 T black tea or 2 T rooibos or tulsi per cup of hot water, strained) preferably cold or room temperature.
½ tsp. Vanilla Powder or ½ bean.
Sweetener of Choice like coconut sugar, sucanat, agave, etc. (optional).

Blend all ingredients together and serve over ice.

<u>Makes: **4 c**   Required: **B**   100% Raw</u>

Green Light

Green and light, an entire salad blended with no need for dressing...saves on time and chewing too!

3 c Mixed Greens like lettuces, kale, dandelion, mustard greens, etc.
2 c *Water Kefir* (p.64)**, *Rejuvelac*** (p.64), or ***Beet Kvass*** (p.66).
Handful of Sprouts like broccoli or sunflower.
1 Celery Stalk
¼-½ Red Bell Pepper
1 Scallion (whole) or up to **¼ Onion**.
4 Sun Dried Tomatoes and/or **1 tsp. Miso** or **Umeboshi Plum Paste**.
½ Lemon juiced.
1 T Flax Oil or **Olive Oil** (optional; beneficial for nutrient absorption).
1 Garlic Clove (optional).
1 Cayenne Pepper or pinch of powder (optional).

Blend till liquefied.

<u>Serves: **2**   Required: **B**   S/F/100% Raw</u>

BEVERAGES (Cold or Warm)

Cold Brewed Coffee

If you just can't say no to Joe, then cold brewing is the way to go! Cold brewing greatly reduces coffee's otherwise acidifying effects. *See "The Sacred Cup" in "Vices made Nicer" chapter for more info.*

2 c Organic Coffee fresh roasted and fresh ground course.
½ G Pure Water

Stir coffee and water together in a half gallon jar, cover with lid or cloth, let sit for 16 hrs., stirring once or twice during, strain through a fine mesh strainer or a cloth/mesh bag into a large bowl, pour liquid concentrate into a clean jar and refrigerate. Use at a rate of about 1 part concentrate per 4 parts hot or cold water. *Keeps in fridge up to 2 weeks.*

Makes: **16± c**   Required: **N/A**   0% Raw

Matcha Latté

Matcha is a high anti-oxidant raw green tea powder that is consumed in its entirety and therefore many times more healthful than other green teas.

1¼ c *Almond Milk* (p.67) or **1 c Pure Water** and **¼ c Almonds***.
1 tsp. Matcha (raw green tea powder).
¼ tsp. Vanilla Powder or ¼ bean.
¼ tsp. Cinnamon (optional).
For a Matcha Mocha Latté: Add **1 T Cacao Powder.**

Blend all ingredients together well, serve over ice or blend longer to make a warmed latte (or start with warm water or slightly heat in a pan). *Matcha should not be heated above 110° or nutrients will be lost.*
*Preferably soaked/sprouted.

Serves: **1**   Required: **B**   S/100% Raw

BEVERAGES (Cold or Warm)

Harmony Chai

2 c **Hot Water**
1 T **Cinnamon**
1-2" **Fresh Ginger** peeled.
1 tsp. **Fennel Seed**
1 tsp. **Coriander Seed**
½ tsp. **Cardamom Powder**
¼ tsp. **Clove Powder**
Pinch of Black Pepper
1 c *Nut/Seed Milk* (p.67) of choice.
1 T **Loose Tea** (black, tulsi, rooibos, etc.).
Sweetener like agave or maple syrup (honey ok if kept below 104°); (optional).

Blend 1 c hot water with spices, add tea, pulse briefly, let sit for 10 min., add remaining cup of hot water (or cold if an iced chai is desired), pulse blend once more, strain through fine strainer, add milk and/or sweetener if desired, serve hot or pour over ice.

Serves: **2**   Required: **B**   S/0% Raw

Mayan Cacao

Decadently delicious!

3 c **Nut Milk** of choice (see recipes p.67).
2 T **Cacao Powder**
1 T **Carob Powder**
2 tsp. **Cinnamon**
Pinch of Nutmeg and **Cayenne Pepper**
Cashew Whip (p.164) or *Coconut Cream Whip* (p.164) (optional).

Blend all ingredients together, serve over ice or heat a bit for a comforting warm drink, top with cool cashew cream if desired.

Serves: **2**   Required: **B**   S/100% Raw

Seasonal Bliss

Instead of offering a bunch of fruit smoothie recipes, we simply suggest blending up whatever fruit is in season and local. The additions below can add extra sustenance and bliss if desired.

Local Seasonal Fruit
Use some frozen if a thicker bliss is desired.
1-2 T Flax and/or **Chia Seeds** sprouted 2-3 days (using terra cotta saucer, see sprouting chapter for details).
Additional ingredients (especially helpful if more liquid is desired):
    1 c Nut Milk of choice (see recipes p.67) or **2-4 Oranges** juiced or **1 Young Thai Coconut** (water & meat) or **1 c *Coconut Yogurt*** (p.76).

Blend all desired ingredients together until smooth and creamy.

Serves: **2**   Required: **B**   S/100% Raw

Pina Colada

Tropically refreshing, especially on tropically hot days. *Coconut water is a rejuvenative full of electrolytes while fruits supply minerals and other restorative nutrients.*

1 Young Thai Coconut (water & meat).
¼-½ Pineapple chopped.
2 Oranges juiced or peel and used whole.
1 Banana frozen.
Ice as needed.

Blend coconut and fruit together until smooth and creamy. Blend in additional ice if desired.

Serves: **2**   Required: **B**   100% Raw

Flying Gorilla

A decedent chocolate banana concoction and a very popular treat at the Healthy Junk booth. *For kids of all ages!*

¾ c **Coconut Water**
1 **Banana** (fresh or frozen).
¼ c **Almonds** *
2-4 **Dates** (optional).
1 T **Cacao Powder**
½-¾ c **Ice** (less if using frozen banana and more when not).

Blend all ingredients together except ice until smooth and creamy, add ice and blend until all is broken and blender runs smooth.
  Preferably soaked/sprouted.

       Serves: **1**   Required: **B**   **S/100**% Raw

Vanilla Date-Nut

Another Healthy Junk booth favorite that keeps'em comen back. *If you like vanilla & creamy, you'll love this one!*

¾ c **Coconut Water**
½ **Banana** (fresh or frozen).
¼ c **Almonds** *
2-4 **Dates**
¼ tsp. **Cinnamon**
¼ tsp. **Vanilla Powder** or ¼ **Bean**.
½-¾ c **Ice** (less if using frozen banana and more when not).

Blend all above ingredients together except for ice until smooth and creamy. Add ice and blend until all ice is broken and blender runs smooth.
  Preferably soaked/sprouted.

       Serves: **1**   Required: **B**   **S/100**% Raw

Brazilian Bliss

A rich and creamy Brazilian delight.

1 ½ c Coconut Water
4-6 Brazil Nuts*
2-4 Dates
1 Banana frozen.
¼ tsp. Vanilla Powder or ¼ bean.
¼ tsp. Cinnamon
Dash of Nutmeg (in or on top).

Blend all ingredients until smooth and creamy.
*Preferably soaked/sprouted.

Serves: **1**   Required: **B**   S/**100**% Raw

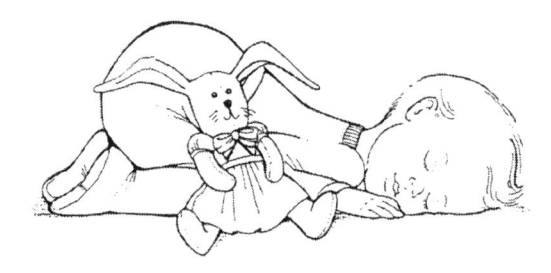

Nighty Night Bliss

A beverage containing some of the best sleep inducing foods known to the Sandman. Almonds and banana both contain magnesium which help relax the muscles and aid in sleep while bananas, peanut butter, and dates (in almond milk) contain L-tryptophan, another powerful sleep aid. *Nutmeg has been proven to be more of a folklore sleep aid than fact...but if you forget you read this it still might work!*

1 ½ c *Almond Milk* (p.67)
1 Banana (fresh or frozen).
1 T *Peanut Butter* (p.131 for ours or use other organic) (optional).
Dash of Nutmeg

Blend until smooth and dreamy!

Serves: **1-2**   Required: **B**   S/**100**% Raw

Breakfast Foods

Real Cereal

Real good, real fresh, real crunchy, real easy, and real satisfying...for real! *Even more kid friendly when allowed to create their own combination.*

Buckwheat (hulled) sprouted and dehydrated.
Apple chopped, or other fresh fruit like pear, peach, apricot, banana, berries, etc.
Raisins or other dried fruit like cranberries, cherries, chopped figs, apples, apricots, or pear, etc.
Sunflower Seeds* and/or **Nuts** like almonds*, hazel nuts*, walnuts*, pecans*, etc. chopped.
Nut/Seed Milk (p.67) of choice.

Optional Additions: Hemp seed, shredded coconut, cinnamon, maple syrup, honey, etc.

Place desired ingredients in bowl and top with milk of choice.

Preferably soaked/sprouted & dehydrated.

Serves: **1+**   Required: **D**   S/**100**% Raw

Coconut Yogurt

A super tasting super culture.

2 Young Thai Coconuts (water & meat).
1 Lime juiced.

Scoop out and place coconut meat in blender with lime juice, blend while pouring just enough coconut water to make consistency thick and creamy, pour mixture into jar, secure with an airtight lid and let sit to ferment at room temperature for 24-48 hrs. *Store unused in fridge.*

Makes: **3+ c**   Required: **B**   F/**100**% Raw

BREAKFAST FOODS

Fruit Seed Porridge

Fruit, seeds, and nuts all come together to get anyone's day off right! *A meal for four small tykes or two big ones!*

Seasonal Fruit (2-3 cups) like figs, peaches, apricots, persimmons, pears, pomegranate, berries, oranges, guavas, cactus pear, etc.
Fruits like fig, persimmon, and mango make porridge naturally thicker as does frozen fruit.
1-2 T Flax*, **Chia*** or **Hemp Seed** or a mix.
½ c *Coconut Yogurt* (p.76) or *Seed Cheese* (p.132) (optional).
¼ c **Dried Fruit** like apple, pear, papaya, apricots, mango, pineapple, cherries, cranberries, blueberries, etc. (optional).
Nuts to top like walnuts**, pecans**, almonds**, etc. (optional).

Blend fruit with seeds, and coconut yogurt if desired, until smooth and creamy, if using add dried fruit and pulse blend to desired chunkiness, top with nuts if desired.

*Preferably sprouted.
**Preferably soaked/sprouted & dehydrated.

Serves: **2-4**   Required: **B**   **S/F/100%** Raw

Max says "it's great!"

Macaw Mash

Some of our Macaw Parrots favorite foods...the like of which might even have you cawing from *your* perch!

1 Banana roughly chopped.
1 Orange roughly chopped.
¼ c **Walnuts*** chopped.
1 Young Thai Coconut (meat only) chopped or *Coconut Yogurt* (p.76).

Place banana, orange and coconut meat or yoghurt together into serving bowls, mash a bit with a fork if desired, top with walnuts.
*Preferably soaked/sprouted & dehydrated.

Serves: **2**   Required: **B**   **100%** Raw

Papaya Boat

This boat has room for two and all the gear!

1 Papaya cut in half and seeded.
Coconut Yogurt (p.76)
Real Cereal (p.76) and/or fresh fruit.

Divide yogurt into papaya halves, top with cereal and/or fresh fruit of choice.

<u>Serves</u>: **2**   Required: **N/A**   <u>S/F/100% Raw</u>

Better Oats

Same good old oatmeal, just one step more to get you more of what you're looking for!

1 c Rolled Oats or **Steel Cut Oats**.
Ferment Starter (1 T rejuvelac, water kefir, apple cider vinegar, or lemon juice combined with 1 c pure water).
1 c Water (in addition to above).
Pinch of Real Salt
Topping(s) of choice: Raisins, banana, dates pieces, or any other dried or fresh fruit, nuts, coconut oil, maple syrup, agave, honey, etc.
Nut/Seed Milk (p.67) of choice.

In a quart jar combine oats with ferment starter, cover with airtight lid and let ferment at room temperature 8-12 hrs. Bring 1 c water to boil, add oat mixture and salt, remove from heat, cover, let sit 5-10 min. (10-15 for steel cut). Top with milk & topping(s) of choice.

<u>Serves</u>: **2**   Required: **N/A**   <u>S/F/20+% Raw</u>

BREAKFAST FOODS

Millet-O-Meal

A hearty breakfast meal in millets!

1 c Millet (hulled; preferably sprouted 1-2 days).
2 c Water
Pinch of Real Salt
Nut/Seed Milk (p.67) of choice.
1 tsp. Coconut Oil (optional).
Sweetener of Choice (optional).

Bring water and salt to a boil, add millet, return to boil, turn heat to low, cover, simmer for 5 minutes, remove from heat and let sit until all liquid is absorbed (about 10 min.), serve with coconut oil and/or sweetener if desired and milk of choice.

Serves: **2**   Required: **N/A**   S/0% Raw

Coconut Cornmeal

1 c Whole Kernel Corn sprouted 1-2 days or Polenta.
Ferment Starter (2 T lime juice combined with 1 c pure water).
2 c Water (in addition to above).
Pinch of Real Salt
2 tsp. Coconut Oil
¼ c Shredded Coconut
Coconut Sugar and/or **Maple Syrup** (optional).
Macadamia Nuts chopped (optional).
Nut/Seed Milk (p.67) of choice.

Blend sprouted corn with ferment starter on low to medium speed till slightly course (skip blending if using Polenta), pour mixture into a quart jar, and cover with airtight lid and let ferment at room temperature for 12-18 hrs. In saucepan bring 2 c water, corn, and salt just to a boil, turn to lowest heat setting, cover and let simmer 15 min., remove from heat, stir in shredded coconut and keep stirring until corn is fully cooked and water has dissipated (about 10 min.), stir in coconut oil, transfer to serving bowls, top with coconut sugar and macadamia nuts if desired and milk of choice.

Serves: **2**   Required: **B**   S/F/10+% Raw

BREAKFAST FOODS

Pancakes

1 c Rolled or **Steel Cut Oats**
Ferment Starter (2 T rejuvelac, water kefir, apple cider vinegar, or lemon juice combined with 1 c pure water).
1 c Buckwheat*
¼ c Almonds*
1½ T Flax Seed
1½ c Water
½ tsp. Real Salt
2 T Coconut Oil

In a jar combine oats with ferment starter, cover with an airtight lid, let sit to ferment at room temperature 12-24 hrs., scoop out into a bowl, blend remaining ingredients and stir into oats, pour ¾ c of batter at a time into a slightly oiled frying pan on med-low heat, spread batter out evenly using a spatula, flip when cooked and firm enough to do so, continue cooking until well done, top as desired with fresh fruit, maple syrup, almond butter, etc.
Preferably soaked/sprouted & dehydrated.

Serves: **4**   Required: **B**   S/F/0% Raw

Pumpkin Pancakes

Pancakes (batter; see recipe above).
1 c Fresh Pumpkin or other **Winter Squash** or **Sweet Potato** shredded.
2 tsp. Cinnamon
½ tsp. Clove
½ tsp. Ginger Powder
½ tsp. Allspice
¼ tsp. Nutmeg
Pecans* and/or **Cranberries** (optional).
Pure Maple Syrup

Stir pumpkin and spices into pancake batter, pour ¾ c of batter at a time into a slightly oiled frying pan on med-low heat, spread batter out evenly using a spatula, flip when cooked and firm enough to do so, continue cooking until well done, top with pecans and/or cranberries and maple syrup if desired.

For Pumpkin Muffins: increase pecans to 1 c and stir into batter along with 1/3 c maple syrup, pour into a muffin pan and bake at 325° for about 35-45 min. or until toothpick comes out clean.
Preferably soaked/sprouted & dehydrated.

Serves: **4**   Required: **B**   S/F/0+% Raw

Apple Spice Pancakes

It's going to be a good day!

Pancakes (batter; see recipe previous page).
1 Apple shredded.
½ c Raisins
2 tsp. Cinnamon
½ tsp. Ginger Powder
½ c Walnuts* chopped (optional).
Pure Maple Syrup

Stir apple, raisins and spices into pancake batter, pour ¾ c of batter at a time into a slightly oiled frying pan on med-low heat, spread batter out evenly using a spatula, flip when cooked and firm enough to do so, continue cooking until well done, top with walnuts and maple syrup if desired.

For Apple Muffins: increase walnuts to 1 cup and stir into batter along with 1/3 cup maple syrup, pour into a muffin pan and bake at 325° for about 35 min. or until toothpick comes out clean.
Preferably soaked/sprouted & dehydrated.

Serves: **4**   Required: **B**   S/F/0+% Raw

Fiji Pancakes

Bula bula!

Pancakes (batter; see recipe previous page).
2 Bananas mashed.
½ c Shredded Coconut (fresh or dried).
1 c Pinneapple chopped.
¼ c Pure Maple Syrup (optional).
½ c Macadamia Nuts chopped (optional).

Stir banana into pancake batter, pour ¾ c of batter at a time into a slightly oiled frying pan on med-low heat, spread batter out evenly using a spatula, sprinkle on 1-2 T shredded coconut, flip pancake when cooked and firm enough to do so, continue cooking until well done, top with pineapple, macadamias, and maple syrup if desired.

For Fiji Muffins: increase macadamia nuts to 1 cup, combine all ingredients, pour into a muffin pan, bake at 325° for about 35 min. or until toothpick comes out clean.

Serves: **4**   Required: **B**   S/F/0+% Raw

Sunrise Dosa

Wake up to a good thing! Hearty without heavy and taste without compromise!

2 *Dosas* (p.113)
1 T Olive Oil or **Coconut Oil**
1 Potato shredded.
¼ Onion diced.
6 Shitake Mushrooms or others sliced.
2 Garlic Cloves minced.
½ Red Bell Pepper diced.
Salt & Pepper to taste.
2 c Spinach
1 Tomato chopped or **Salsa**.
Avocado sliced or chopped.
Cilantro chopped (optional).

While dosas cook per recipe instructions, heat oil in a large sauce pan and cook potato, onion, mushrooms and garlic on medium heat. As soon as potatoes brown, stir in bell pepper, salt and pepper, a minute later stir in spinach, when wilted and bright green scoop mixture onto dosas, add any optional ingredients, fold and serve.

Serves: **2**   Required: **N/A**   S/F/5% Raw

Snacks

Cauliflower Popcorn

Pop-popular at the Healthy Junk booth, mostly because people don't know what to expect and just have to give it a try...again and again! *Below is our standard spice mix but feel free to add or substitute seasonings and spices for variety.*

1 Cauliflower Head cut into bite sized pieces.
¼ c Olive Oil
2 T Nutritional Yeast
½ tsp. Real Salt
2-3 Cloves Garlic pressed or minced or 1 tsp. garlic powder.
¼-¾ tsp. Chili Powder depending on heat of powder and desire.

Place cauliflower pieces in serving bowls, whisk remaining ingredients together in a bowl with a fork, drizzle onto cauliflower.

Serves: **4-6**   Required: **N/A**   95% Raw

Better Popcorn

Quality oil and nutritional yeast for healthy buttery flavor along with real salt makes this popcorn "to live for"!

½ c Popcorn
2 T Coconut Oil
¼ c Flax Oil or **Olive Oil**
2 T Nutritional Yeast
Real Salt
Spices of choice: like chili powder, cayenne pepper, fresh pressed garlic or garlic powder, onion powder, chipolte powder, sage powder, kelp or dulse flakes, all purpose seasoning, etc.

Place coconut oil and popcorn in a wok or large pot on high heat and cover, remove from heat as soon as bulk of popping has subsides, lift lid slightly to let out steam and hold until popping seizes, transfer to serving bowls, drizzle or spray on flax or olive oil, stir to coat, sprinkle on nutritional yeast, salt, and desired spices.

Serves: **2-4**   Required: **N/A**   0% Raw

Chickpea Fries

Crispy soft, salty, and slightly oily, but no clown!

1 c Chickpeas (garbanzo beans) sprouted 2 days.
3 c Water
1 T Olive Oil
Real Salt to taste.
Optional Spices: garlic (fresh pressed or powder), onion powder, chili powder, nutritional yeast, etc.

In sauce pan bring chickpeas and water to a boil, turn to low, cover and simmer till well done, drain, stir in olive oil, salt, and desired spices to coat, transfer to a shallow baking pan and bake at 350° in pre-heated oven (fan bake if you have the option), when slightly browned (about 8 min.) stir chickpeas around a bit then cook till slightly browned and crispy (8 min. more). Eat as is or with *Ketchup* and/or *Mustard*.

<u>Serves</u>: **2**   Required: **N/A**   S/0% Raw

Onion Rings

The real deal! Don't forget the *Ketchup (p. 144)*!

½ c Chickpea Flour (preferably from sprouted & dehydrated chickpeas).
½+ c Water
1 T Grapeseed, Canola, or **Coconut Oil**
½ tsp. each **Onion Powder, Garlic Powder,** and **Real Salt**
½ tsp. Chili Powder (optional).
1 Onion (preferably a sweet variety) sliced and separated into rings.

Whisk together all ingredients except onion, drag or dip rings of onion through batter, place on oiled cookie sheet, and bake at 400° until golden (about 15 min.).

<u>Serves</u>: **2-4**   Required: **N/A**   0% Raw

Sesame Rice Crackers

Thin, crisp, and slightly chewy.

1 c Short Grain Brown Rice sprouted 2-3 days.
1¼ c Water
1 c Sesame Seeds (un-hulled) sprouted 2-3 days.
1 T Sesame Oil
2 tsp. Real Salt or **¼ c Nama Shoyu** or **Tamari**

Bring water and rice to a boil, turn stove to lowest heat setting, cover and simmer till rice is tender (about 20 min.). Preheat oven to 350°. In a food processor process rice, oil, salt, and just enough water to process into a thick batter, add sesame seeds and pulse to mix. Roll batter into teaspoon size balls and place on oiled cookie sheet, oil a small piece of parchment or wax paper, place oil side down on balls of dough and flatten with the bottom side of a cup until very thin. Bake until crisp (about 15-30 min.).

<u>Makes: **24±**</u>   Required: **FP**   S/0% Raw

Crispy Crackers

2 c Sesame Seeds (un-hulled) sprouted 2-3 days.
2 c Flax Seeds soaked 6 hrs. in **1½ c Pure Water** (do not rinse).
1 T Miso
Optional Herbs & Spices: fresh or dried basil, oregano, thyme, sage, garlic, garlic powder, onion powder, etc.

Blend sesame seeds and miso with just enough water to blend well, add flax seed and blend just to mix. *Fermenting optional but recommended by transferring to a bowl then covering with cloth and letting sit at room temperature for 8-24 hrs.* Mix in any desired herbs and/or spices, spread onto teflex sheets ¼" thick, score and dehydrate at 110° for 10 hrs., flip directly onto dehydrator trays, remove teflex sheets, dehydrate until crisp (about 10 hrs. more).

<u>Serves: **16±**</u>   Required: **B & D**   S/F/100% Raw

SNACKS

Mineral Crunch Bars

A sweet, salty, crunchy snack treat loaded with calcium and minerals.

1½ c Sesame Seeds (un-hulled) soaked 8-12 hrs. and rinsed.
¼ c Dried Seaweed like kombu, wakame, kelp, "sea crunchies", etc. crumbled, scissor cut, or flaked.
¼ c Maple Syrup or **Agave Nectar**

Mix all ingredients together in a bowl, spread onto a teflex sheet about ¼" thick, score to desired size and dehydrate at 110° until crunchy but still flexible (about 12-18 hrs.).

Makes: **20±**   Required: **D**   S/**80**% Raw

SNACKS (Dehydrated)

Seasoned Almonds

Satisfy most any craving at any time when this snack is on hand.

2 lbs. Almonds soaked 12 hrs. then drained and rinsed thoroughly.
1½ c Nutritional Yeast
¼ c Miso, Tamari, or **Nama Shoyu** (contains wheat).
2 T Olive Oil
1 Lemon juiced.
Optional additions to sauce: fresh or dried onion, garlic, peppers, soaked sun dried tomatoes, herbs, seasonings, etc.

Blend all ingredients except almonds into a thick sauce, adding water if needed to blend, in a large bowl stir sauce with almonds to coat, spread onto dehydrator trays in single layers and dehydrate at 110° until dry and crunchy (about 3 days).

Makes: **2 lbs.**   Required: **B & D**   S/**100**% Raw

SNACKS (Dehydrated)

Sweet & Spicy Walnuts

A compliment of sweet, spicy and crunchy makes these guys impressive & irresistible.

4 c Walnuts soaked 12 hrs. then drained and rinsed well (also best to let dry out for ½ a day or so...so that coating sticks better).
¼ c Maple Syrup or **Agave**
½ tsp. Vanilla Powder or ½ bean.
¼ tsp. Real Salt
2 T Chili Pepper Flakes or **¼ tsp. Cayenne Powder** or other dried hot pepper ground.

Mix all ingredients together in a bowl until walnuts are well coated, spread onto dehydrator trays in single layers, dehydrate at 110° until dry and crunchy (24+ hrs.).

Makes: **4 c**   Required: **D**   S/95% Raw

Chili-Lime Pistachios

Spicy and sour...ooh yah! *Pistachios are one of only a few higher alkalizing nuts.*

2 c Pistachios soaked 4 hrs. then drained and rinsed.
1 bunch fresh **Cilantro**
1 Lime juiced.
1½ T Chili Powder
¼ c Miso, Tamari, or **Nama Shoyu** (contains wheat).

Mix all ingredients together in a bowl until pistachios are well coated, spread onto dehydrator trays in single layers, dehydrate at 110° until dry and crunchy (24+ hrs.).

Makes: **2 c**   Required: **D**   S/100% Raw

SNACKS (Dehydrated)

Green Seeds

Awesome salty crunchy nutritional snack to have around. Provides chlorophyll, usable calcium, protein, etc. *Also excellent sprinkled on salads.*

4 c Sunflower Seeds (hulled) sprouted 1-2 days.
½ - ¾ c Pure Water
¼ c Spirulina or **Chlorella** or combo.
1 c Nutritional Yeast
1 Lime juiced.
½ Onion chopped or 1 tsp. onion powder.
½-1 T Real Salt or **¼-1½ tsp. Himalayan Sea Salt**
½ tsp. Chipotle Powder
2 T Olive Oil (optional).

Blend all but sunflower seeds until a thick creamy sauce is formed, in a large bowl pour batter over seeds and stir well, spread into single layers onto dehydrator trays and dehydrate at 110° until dry and crunchy (about 24 hrs.).

<u>Makes:</u> **4 c**   <u>Required:</u> **B & D**   **S/100% Raw**

Veggie Munch

8-12 c Vegetables like onions and bell peppers sliced thin, or zucchini, carrots, beets, etc. julienne cut.
 Or **3 bunches Kale** de-stemmed.
<u>Sauce:</u>
1½ c Nutritional Yeast
¼ c Miso, Tamari, or **Nama Shoyu** (contains wheat).
2 T Olive Oil
1 Lemon juiced.
1 c Cashews, Sunflower or **Pumpkin Seeds** (optional).
<u>**Other optional sauce additions:**</u> Fresh or dried onion, garlic, peppers, soaked sun dried tomatoes, herbs, seasonings, etc.

Blend all ingredients except fresh veggies to form a sauce, adding water if needed, in large bowl stir sauce with veggies, spread into single layers onto dehydrator trays, dehydrate at 110° until dry and crunchy (10-36 hours, depending on veggies).

<u>Makes:</u> **6 c**   <u>Required:</u> **B & D**   **100% Raw**

SNACKS (Dehydrated)

Apple Chewla

An Apple Chewla a day keeps the doctor away!

4 Apples cored and sliced.
¾ c Walnuts or **Pecans** soaked 12 hrs. and rinsed..
1 T Fresh Ginger grated.
½ Lemon juiced.
2 tsp. Cinnamon
¼ tsp. Real Salt

Place all ingredients in a food processor and pulse until mixture is diced into small but recognizable pieces, scoop spoonfuls of mixture onto teflex sheet and flatten to about 3/8", dehydrate at 110° for 8 hrs., flip onto dehydrating trays, remove teflex sheet, dehydrate until dry and chewy (about 10-12 hrs. more).

Makes: **3+ c**   Required: **FP & D**   S/**100%** Raw

Hula Chewla

A chewly nutty taste of the tropics!

1 c Young Thai Coconut Meat
2 c Fresh Pineapple cut into chunks.
2 c Banana sliced into chunks.
1 c Macadamia Nuts or **Brazil Nuts** soaked 6-8 hrs., drained & rinsed.
½ Lemon juiced.
½ tsp. Vanilla Powder or ½ bean.
¼ tsp. Real Salt

Place all ingredients in food processor and pulse until mixture is diced into small but recognizable pieces, scoop spoonfuls of mixture onto teflex sheet and flatten to about 3/8", dehydrate at 110° for 8 hrs., flip onto dehydrating trays, remove teflex sheet, dehydrate until dry and chewy (about 10-12 hrs. more).

Makes: **3-4 c**   Required: **FP & D**   S/**100%** Raw

Salads & Dressings

Plop Top Salad

The basic veggie portion makes a good salad on its own, but if it's a hearty meal your after simply plop on one of the choices below.

Mixed Greens
Onion chopped.
Broccoli Sprouts
Seasonal Veggies
Avocado sliced or chopped (optional).
Dressing of Choice

<u>Plop of Choice:</u>
Seed Cheese (p.132)
Med Spread (p.132)
Sunflower Hummus (p.135)
Bandito Dip (p.140)
Hummus (not raw) (p.135).
Sloppy Jose's filling (not raw) (p.128).

Throw greens on plates, add dressing of choice, plop on plop of choice, *chew each bite thoroughly...*

<u>Serves</u>: **?**   <u>Required</u>: **N/A**   **S/100%** Raw

Caesar Salad

A healthier Caesar...long live the Emperor in all of us!

1 Head Romaine Lettuce chopped.
¼ Red Onion sliced thin.
¼ c Pine Nuts
8 Kalamata Olives
1 Lemon juiced.
½ c Olive Oil
2-4 Garlic Cloves
¼-½ tsp. Kelp Flakes
½ tsp. Cumin Powder
½ tsp. Real Salt
½ tsp. Pepper

Place all ingredients except lettuce and red onion into a blender and blend until smooth and creamy. Place roughly chopped lettuce into a large bowl and toss with dressing and onion slices.

<u>Serves</u>: **4**   <u>Required</u>: **B**   **100%** Raw

Far East Coleslaw

1 Head Cabbage shredded.
2 Large Carrots grated.
¼ Onion (yellow or white) shredded.
1 Celery Root grated (optional).
1 T Umeboshi Plum Paste
2 T Sesame Oil
1 T Agave or **Honey**
½ c Sesame Seeds (un-hulled).

Toast sesame seeds by stirring in a hot skillet on medium heat till crunchy and aromatic (about 5 min.). In large bowl combine cabbage, celery root, and carrot, in a small bowl and with the use of a fork, mash onion, plum paste, sesame oil, and agave together well, stir along with sesame seeds into veggies.

Serves: **10+**   Required: **N/A**   F/**100**% Raw

Cool Hand Cuke

Cucumbers, mint and lemon are all cooling foods, making this one of the *coolest* dishes around!

2 Cucumbers spiralized or shredded into noodles.
1-2 T Mint Leaves
¼ c Pine Nuts or **Macadamia Nuts**
¼ c Onion (preferably sweet white).
1 Lime juiced.
1 T Olive Oil
Real Salt to taste.

Blend ¼ cup of cucumber noodles with all other ingredients. In a bowl pour mixture over remaining noodles, toss and serve.

Serves: **2**   Required: **B**   **100**% Raw

Whole Beet Salad

Steamed beets and their greens, surprising delicious and satisfying when tossed into a fresh green salad!

Mixed Salad Greens
1 Bunch Beets (about 4, with tops).
¼ Onion thinly sliced or chopped.
12 Garlic Cloves (optional).
Salad Dressing of choice.

Slice beet roots into bite size wedges and start steaming along with cloves of garlic if using. Roughly cut beet stems and leaves but keep separate. Just as beats start to turn soft, add stem pieces, 2-3 minutes later add leaf pieces, cook 2-3 minutes more, place on top of salad greens and mix in a bit, top with onions and dressing of choice.

Serves: **2-4**   Required: **N/A**   **50**% Raw

Hot Head

A combo of spicy hot and steamed hot to warm things up.

1 Cabbage Head
2 T Miso mixed with **1 T Water, Tamari,** or **Nama Shoyu** (contains wheat).
1 T Sesame Seeds (un-hulled).
1 T Chili Pepper Flakes

Cut core portion from cabbage, cut into 6-8 wedges and steam until tender. While cabbage cooks toast sesame seeds by stirring in a hot skillet on medium heat till crunchy and aromatic (about 5 min.). In a large bowl mix cabbage with Nama Shoyu, sesame seeds, and chili pepper flakes until cabbage partially breaks apart.

Serves: **6**   Required: **N/A**   **F/0+**% Raw

SALADS

Confetti Salad

Mixed Salad Greens
1 c Adzuki Beans sprouted 3-4 days.
2 Corn Ears kernels removed.
2 Tomatoes diced.
1 Cucumber diced.
1 Avocado diced.
1 Red Bell diced.
¼ Onion diced.
½ c Cilantro chopped.
1+ Fresh Hot Pepper such as anaheim, jalapeño, chipotle, serrano, etc. minced.
1 Lime juiced.
Chili Powder to taste.
Real Salt to taste.

Cook beans by boiling in 3 c water turning to low and simmering till beans are soft. In a large bowl stir all ingredients together except avocado, lightly stir in avocado, scoop over beds of salad greens.

Serves: **2**   Required: **N/A**   80% Raw

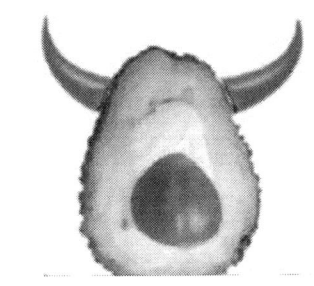

Deviled Avos

A devilish tasty concoction providing pro-biotics, B vitamins, healthy fats, and more!

2 Avocados cut in half lengthwise and seed removed.
1 c *Sauerkraut* (p.145 for ours or use other).
1 T *Mustard* (p.144 for ours or use other).
1-2 T Nutritional Yeast
Smoked Paprika or **Paprika**
Broccoli or **Sunflower Sprouts**

Stir mustard into Sauerkraut, scoop onto avocado halves, lay on some sprouts, sprinkle on nutritional yeast and paprika.

Serves: **2**   Required: **N/A**   F/95% Raw

SALAD DRESSINGS

Raw Ranch

2 c *Seed Cheese* (p.140) or **1 c Macadamia** or **Cashews** soaked 1-2 hrs.
½ **Lemon** juiced.
¼ **c Apple Cider Vinegar**
¼ **c Olive Oil**
½ **Onion** (preferably sweet variety).
2 Garlic Cloves
1-2 Dates (1 if Medjool) soaked if not already soft.
1 T Fresh Dill
1 T Fresh Parsley
1 T Fresh or **Dried Chives**
1 T Miso (preferably mellow white).
1 tsp. Dried Basil

Blend all ingredients until smooth and creamy, adding water for desired consistency.

Makes: **2 c**   Required: **B**   S/F/**100**% Raw

Date Dijon

Dates are used to make a vegan version of the more common Honey Dijon, but honey can be substituted if desired. Water can be used in place of oil as well.

1 Red Bell Pepper chopped.
1 Celery Stalk chopped.
½ **Onion** (preferably sweet) chopped.
4 Dates (2 if medjool) or 2 T honey.
½ **c Olive Oil** or **Pure Water**
1 Lemon juiced.
2+ Garlic Cloves
2 T *Mustard* (p.144 for ours or use other).
1 tsp. Dulse or **Kelp Flakes** or **Powder**.

Blend all ingredients together until smooth and creamy.

Makes: **1+ c**   Required: **B**   **100**% Raw

SALAD DRESSINGS

Yeast Ahoy!

One of our favorites...that yeast is addicting! *Nutritional yeast lives up to its name as it is high in protein and many of the B vitamins, including B-12.*

1 c **Olive Oil**
½ c **Nutritional Yeast**
1 **Lemon** juiced.
1" **Chunk Ginger** peeled.
2 **Garlic Cloves**
2 T **Miso, Tamari,** or **Nama Shoyu** (contains wheat).
1 T **Apple Cider Vinegar**

Blend all ingredients together until smooth and creamy.

<u>Makes:</u> **2 c**   Required: **B**   F/80% Raw

Sesame Ginger

Our *current* favorite dressing. Can be made oil free if desired and still provide a bounty of flavor. Also good on veggie sandwiches, drizzled over our *Looky Like Sushi Roll,* etc.

¼ c **Sesame Seeds** (un-hulled).
1"+ **Chunk Ginger** peeled.
3 tsp. **Miso, Tamari,** or **Nama Shoyu** (contains wheat).
1 T **Agave** or **Honey**
1-2 **Garlic Cloves**
¼ **Onion**
½ **Lemon** juiced.
1 T **Apple Cider Vinegar**
½ c **Olive Oil** or **Water**

Toast sesame seeds by stirring in a hot skillet on medium heat till crunchy and aromatic (about 5 min.), blend with all other ingredients until smooth and creamy.

<u>Makes:</u> **1+ c**   Required: **B**   F/90% Raw

SALAD DRESSINGS

Cilantro Avo

A fresh taste of creamy for your greens...with optional heat!

1 Avocado
½ c Olive Oil
1 Lime juiced.
1 Orange juiced.
1 Green Onion
1 Bunch Fresh Cilantro destemmed.
1 Hot Chili Pepper seeded...or not if you like it hot! (optional).
½ tsp. Real Salt
Dash of Black Pepper

Blend all ingredients until smooth and creamy.

Makes: **2 c**   Required: **B**   **100**% Raw

Two Tomato Herb

A rich and bold double dose of tomato dressing.

2 Tomatoes (med.-large) quartered.
10 Kalamata Olives pitted.
½ c Sun Dried Tomatoes soaked 15+ min. in just enough water to cover.
¼ c Olive Oil
¼ Onion chopped.
2+ Garlic Cloves
¼ c Fresh Basil or **Tarragon** or 1 T dried.
1 T Miso

Blend all ingredients, including sun dried tomato soak water, until smooth and creamy.

Makes: **2+ c**   Required: **B**   **F/100**% Raw

SALAD DRESSINGS

Tahini Dressing

Besides being tasty on a salad this dressing is great for dipping, drizzling on our *Falafels*, etc.

½ c **Sesame Seeds** (un-hulled) sprouted 2-3 days.
½ c+ **Pure Water**
¼ c **Olive Oil**
2 **Garlic Cloves**
1-2 **Dates** or 1 T **Honey**
½ **Lemon** juiced.
2 T **Miso, Tamari,** or **Nama Shoyu** (contains wheat).

Toast sesame seeds by stirring in a hot skillet on medium heat till crunchy and aromatic (about 5 min.). Blend all ingredients until smooth, adding water to desired consistency. Taste, adjust as desired.

Makes: **1½ c**   Required: **B**   S/**100**% Raw

Creamy Kraut

We have found exciting flavor when sauerkraut is combined with mustard and take full advantage of it here.

1 c *Sauerkraut* (including liquid) (p.145 for ours or use other).
1 **Avocado**
2 T **Nutritional Yeast**
2-3 **Garlic Cloves**
2 T *Mustard* (p.144 for ours or use other).
1 tsp. **All Purpose Seasoning** or dried herbs of choice.

Blend all ingredients until smooth and creamy.

Makes: **2 c**   Required: **B**   F/**100**% Raw

SALAD DRESSINGS

Mustard Curry

May your salad never be bored with dressing again!

¾ c **Olive Oil**
½ c *Beet Kvass* (p.66)
1 **Lemon** juiced.
2-3 **Garlic Cloves**
1 T **Curry Powder**
2 T *Mustard* (p.144 for ours or use other).

Blend all ingredients until smooth and creamy.

Makes: **2+ c**   Required: **B**   F/**100**% Raw

Herb Goddess

A flavorful herb filled dressing. If missing a few herbs on the list, it'll still turn out...but must be demoted to Herb God!

1 c *Sauercream* (p.134)
1 **Tomato**
3 **Scallions** (white & green parts).
2-3 **Garlic Cloves**
¼ c **Fresh Basil**
2 T **Fresh Tarragon**
2 T **Fresh Chives**
1 T **Fresh Parsley**
1 tsp. **Dulse** or **Kelp Flakes** or **Powder**.
1 **Lemon** juiced.
½ tsp. **Black Pepper**

Blend all ingredients until smooth and creamy.

Makes: **2 c**   Required: **B**   S/F/**100**% Raw

Soups

Better Broth

This vegan broth can be used in place of chicken or vegetable broth or bouillon...and you won't even miss them!

Per 4-6 c Water use:
¼-½ c **Nutritional Yeast**
¼ c **Olive Oil**
Real Salt or **Himalayan Salt** to taste.

After soup is cooked and stove is off, stir in yeast, oil, and salt, let sit for 10-15 minutes before serving.

Makes: **4-6 c** Required: **N/A** **0**+% Raw

Bloody Good Soup

Raw, red, and rich in flavor and nutrition.

2 **Large Tomatoes** diced.
1 **Medium Cucumber** diced.
2 **Celery Stalks**
1 **Lemon** juiced.
1 T **Miso** (preferably red).
2 **Fresh Cayenne Peppers** or powder to taste.
½ tsp. **Black Pepper**

Optional Toppings: avocado, cucumber, sweet onion, zucchini, celery, red bell pepper, cilantro, basil, parsley, etc. diced.

Blend ingredients until smooth and creamy, add optional toppings as desired.

Serves: **2** Required: **B** **F/100**% Raw

Allium Soup

A soup for alliums...garlic and onion lovers!

1 Onion (yellow or white) diced.
8-10 Garlic Cloves sliced or diced.
2 Celery Stalks sliced.
1 T Olive Oil
4 c Pure Water
2 Potatoes (Red, Yukon Gold, or similar) diced.
1 Large Carrot diced.
¼ Head Cabbage shredded/chopped.
1 T Fresh Thyme or 1 tsp. dried.
½ tsp. Pepper
2 T Miso
¼ c Nutritional Yeast
2 T Fresh Parsley chopped fine (optional).

In large pot on medium heat sauté onion, garlic and celery in oil just till soft, stir in water, potato, carrot, cabbage, thyme and pepper, cover and let come to a boil, turn to low and simmer until potato and carrot are soft, remove from heat uncover and let cool about 10 min., using a ladle transfer half of the soup to a blender, add miso and yeast, blend briefly, pour back into pot and stir, ladle into bowls and serve garnished with parsley if desired.

Serves: **2-3**   Required: **B**   F/0% Raw

SOUPS

Tomato Curry

1 Young Thai Coconut (meat & water) or **1½ c Pure Water** and **1 Avocado**.
4 Tomatoes (med.) chopped.
2 Bell Peppers (any color but green) chopped.
½ Onion (white or yellow) chopped.
2 Celery Stalks
2" Chunk Ginger peeled.
¼ c Cilantro chopped.
1 Lemon juiced.
3 Garlic Cloves
1 T Maple Syrup, Agave, or **Honey**
¼ c Miso, Tamari, or **Nama Shoyu** (contains wheat).
1 T Curry Powder
Cayenne Powder to taste (optional).

Blend all ingredients until smooth and creamy.

Serves: **2-3**   Required: **B**   F/**100**% Raw

Pumpkin Chestnut

Fall never tasted so good!

10-12 Chestnuts
6 c Water
1 Pumpkin (med.) chopped.
1 Onion chopped.
8 Garlic Cloves halved.
2 Bay Leaves
2 T Fresh Tarragon or 2 tsp. dried.
¼-½ tsp. Black Pepper
¼ tsp. Mace or **Nutmeg**
¼ c Nutritional Yeast
Real Salt to taste.

Cut X into skin of chestnut shells, boil in 2 c water for 3 min., remove from heat, take a few out at a time and peel off shells (harder to peel as they cool). In a large pot boil 4 c water, add chestnuts and remaining ingredients except yeast and salt, cover, turn down and simmer till pumpkin is soft and mushy, remove from heat, stir in yeast and salt, let stand 10 min., blend ½ - ¾ of the mixture and add back to pot, stir and serve.

Serves: **4**   Required: **B**   **0**% Raw

SOUPS

Hot Pot

1 T Black Sesame Seeds (un-hulled).
1 T Sesame Oil or **Olive Oil**
2 c Shitake Mushrooms sliced.
3-5 Garlic Cloves sliced.
¼-½ tsp. Crushed Red Pepper
2 Small Bok Choy chopped (stems and greens seperated).
5 c *Better Broth* (p.102)
1 c Kelp Noodles
2 Large Carrots shredded.
2 T Fresh Ginger grated.
2 Scallions sliced thin.
1 Lemon juiced.
¼ c Miso, Tamari, or **Nama Shoyu** (contains wheat).

Toast sesame seeds by stirring in a hot skillet on medium heat till crunchy and aromatic (about 5 min.). In soup pot sauté mushrooms, garlic, red pepper and bok choy stems in 1 T oil on medium heat till soft, stir in remaining ingredients (including sesame seeds), cover, just as soup reaches a simmer remove from heat and serve.

Serves: **4-5**   Required: **N/A**   **0%** Raw

Frijoles Soup

Mmmm them's good beans!

1 c Red Beans or other sprouted 3-4 days.
3 c Water
½ Onion chopped.
3 Garlic Cloves minced
1-2 tsp. Chili Powder
½ tsp. Cumin Powder
1 tsp. Oregano Powder
1 Dried Pepper of Choice crushed or ground (optional).
Red Bell Pepper diced.
Tomato diced.
Avocado diced.
Cilantro chopped.
1 Lime

In a soup pot bring beans and water to a boil, turn to low cover and simmer until almost soft, add onion, garlic and spices (including dried pepper if using), when beans are soft and no longer boney remove from heat and transfer to serving bowls, top with bell pepper, tomato, avocado, cilantro, and a squeeze of lime juice.

Serves: **2**   Required: **N/A**   **10+%** Raw

SOUPS

Legumenous Soup

1 c each **Lentils**, **Adzuki** and **Mung Beans** sprouted together 2-4 days.
6 c **Pure Water**
2 **Bay Leaves**
1 **White Onion** diced.
2 **Carrots** diced.
4 **Garlic Cloves** pressed or minced.
2 **Tomatoes** diced.
8 **Kale Leaves** destemmed and chopped.
¼ - ½ c **Nutritional Yeast**
2 T **Olive Oil**
Real Salt to taste.

In a soup pot bring beans, water, and bay leaves to a boil, turn to low cover and simmer until legumes are almost soft, add onion, carrot, garlic and yeast, bring back to boil, turn off heat, add kale cover and let sit 15 min., stir in olive oil and salt and serve.

Serves: **6+**   Required: **N/A**   **S/0**+% Raw

Summer Squash

1 c **Basmati** or **Jasmine Rice***
4½ c **Water**
6 c **Zucchini**, **Crookneck**, or **Patty Pan Squash** sliced or chopped.
1 **Red Onion** sliced thin.
1 **Red**, **Yellow**, or **Orange Bell Pepper** julienne sliced.
4-8 **Garlic Cloves** sliced or diced.
2 T **Olive Oil**
1 tsp. **Paprika**
½ tsp. **Real Salt**
½ tsp. **Black Pepper**
2 **Large Tomatoes** chopped.
¼ c **Nutritional Yeast**
½ c **Basil** chopped.
1 **Lemon** juiced.

Cook rice by boiling with 1½ c water then simmering till tender (about 20 min.). In a large soup pot sauté squash along with onion, pepper and garlic in olive oil on medium heat until squash is crisp tender, sprinkle on paprika, salt and pepper, stir and sauté another minute, stir in remaining 3 c water, yeast, basil, and lemon juice, then stir in rice and tomato, cover and bring just to a simmer then serve.
*Preferably sprouted.

Serves: **3-4**   Required: **N/A**   **S/0**% Raw

Broccauli

Easy nutritious cool weather soup. Suggest serving with *Chipati* for dipping.

5 Red Potatoes sliced thin.
6 c Water
3-4 c Broccoli cut and broken into florets and stems chopped.
3-4 c Cauliflower cut and broken into florets and stems chopped.
½-1 Onion chopped.
3-4 Garlic Cloves sliced or diced (optional).
½ c Nutritional Yeast
¼ c Olive Oil
Salt & **Pepper** to taste.

In a large soup pot on medium heat cook potatoes in water till tender, break up with whisk, add broccoli, cauliflower, onion, garlic and nutritional yeast, turn to low and cook till tender, remove from heat, whisk in olive oil, salt and pepper.

Serves: **4-6**   Required: **N/A**   0% Raw

Cauliflower Curry

4 c Cauliflower chopped and steamed (use uncooked for raw soup).
1 Young Thai Coconut (water & meat).
2 Celery Stalks roughly chopped.
1 Red Bell Pepper roughly chopped.
4 Garlic Cloves
1 Lemon juiced.
2 T Curry Powder
Cashews
Cilantro chopped.

Blend all but cashews and cilantro till smooth and creamy, garnish with cashews and cilantro.

Serves: **3-4**   Required: **B**   20-100% Raw

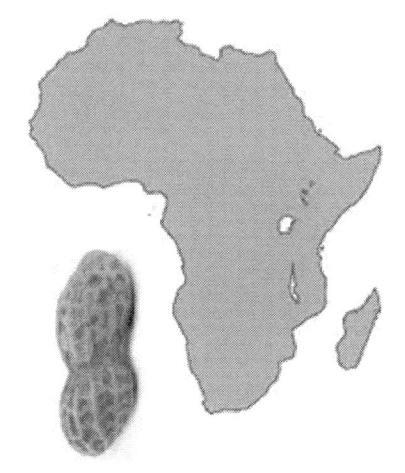

African Peanut Stew

Creamy, spicy, peanutty, and easy...no wonder their dancin over there!

1 T Coconut Oil
½ Onion (yellow or white) diced.
3-5 Garlic Cloves minced.
3 c Pure Water
2 Sweet Potatoes cubed.
½ c Chickpeas sprouted 2-3 days.
½ c *Peanut Butter* (p.131 for ours or use other organic).
2 T Fresh Ginger grated.
1 T Coriander Seed ground.
1 tsp. Cumin Powder
1-2 tsp. Red Pepper Flakes crushed or ground.
1 tsp. Real Salt
1 Bunch Collard Greens chopped.
2 Tomatoes diced.

In a soup pot over medium heat sauté onion and garlic in oil just till soft, add water, sweet potato and chickpeas, cover and let come to a boil, turn to low and simmer just till sweet potato and chickpeas turn soft, stir in peanut butter and spices until well mixed, stir in collard greens, cover and simmer 5 more minutes, stir in tomatoes.

Serves: **3-4**   Required: **N/A**   **S/0**% Raw

Main Meals

MAIN MEALS (Accessories)

Seed Crusts

Soft but sturdy crusts that can be used for open face sandwiches, pizzas, spreads, dips, etc.

2 c Sunflower Seeds (hulled) sprouted 1-2 days.
½ c Flax Seed ground.
¼ c Miso, Tamari, or **Nama Shoyu** (contains wheat).
1 c Pure Water warmed.
3 Garlic Cloves pressed or minced.
2 T Olive Oil

In a food processor process sunflower seeds until fine, dissolve miso in warm water and stir in flax, add mixture along with remaining ingredients to food processor and process with seeds until well mixed, spread onto teflex sheets to a thickness of ¼", score to desired size and dehydrate at 110° for 10 hrs., flip onto trays, remove teflex sheets, dehydrate until crusts are dry but flexible (12+ hrs.).

Makes: **16±**   Required: **FP & D**   S/F/**100**% Raw

Veggie Seed Crusts

Like *Seed Crusts* but more herbs, veggies, and savory.

2 c Sunflower Seeds (hulled) sprouted 1-2 days.
½ c Flax Seed ground.
¼ c Miso, Tamari, or **Nama Shoyu** (contains wheat).
1 c Pure Water warmed.
1 c Red Bell Pepper shredded.
1 c Onion shredded.
1 c Carrot shredded.
1 c Celery shredded.
6 Garlic Cloves pressed or minced.
¼ c Fresh Basil chopped or 2 T dry.

In a food processor process sunflower seeds until fine, dissolve miso in warm water and stir in flax, add mixture along with remaining ingredients to food processor and process with seeds until well mixed, spread onto teflex sheets to a thickness of ¼", score to desired size and dehydrate at 110° for 10 hrs., flip onto trays, remove teflex sheets, dehydrate until crusts are dry but flexible (12+ hrs.).

Makes: **16±**   Required: **FP & D**   S/F/**100**% Raw

Chickpea Noodles

Fast homemade gluten free noodles to use in a variety of dishes.

1¾ c Chickpea Flour (preferably from sprouted and dehydrated chickpeas).
2 T Flax Seed ground.
6 T Warm Water

In a small bowl stir flax with water and set aside for 10 min. Place chickpea flour on a cutting board and form a well in the middle, pour flax mixture in well, knead together with hands until a dough forms, wrap in plastic wrap and let sit at room temperature for 30 min., divide dough into 2-4 pieces, roll out very thin on a floured surface, slice into desired size noodles, cook by dropping noodles into a pot of rapidly boiling water for 2-3 min. or until pasta is cooked through, drain and serve as desired.

Serves: **3-4**   Required: **N/A**   **0**% Raw

MAIN MEALS (Accessories)

Tortillas

You won't find a healthier or tastier tortilla this side of the boarder...or the other side come to think of it!

1 c **Whole Kernel Corn** combined with **1 T Flax Seed** and sprouted 2-3 days.
1 c **Pure Water**
2 T **Fresh Squeezed Lime Juice** or ½ tsp. **Miso**
½ tsp. **Real Salt**

Blend sprouted corn and flax with water and lime juice or miso, pour into quart jar, cover with air tight lid, let sit to ferment at room temperature for 12-24 hrs., stir in salt, pour batter in thin layers onto a non-stick skillet over medium heat, flip when top appears dry and tortilla is firm enough to do so, remove when firm and cooked through. Refrigerate unused cooked tortillas or batter for later use.

Makes: **4-6**   Required: **B**   S/F/0% Raw

Chapati

Hearty flat bread cooked and used as a shell for other foods or served with soups or saucy dishes for dipping.

½ c each **Millet***, **Amaranth***, and **Whole Kernel Corn*** and **1 T Flax Seed** blended or ground into flour.
1 c **Pure Water**
2 T **Coconut Oil**
½ tsp. **Real Salt**

In a bowl stir all ingredients together to form a thick batter, roll into 6 equal sized balls, flatten to 1/8" and place into a non-stick skillet over medium heat, flip when top appears dry and chapati is firm enough to do so, remove when firm and cooked through. Refrigerate unused cooked chapatis or batter for later use.

Preferably sprouted & dehydrated.

Makes: **6**   Required: **B**   S/0% Raw

MAIN MEALS (Accessories)

Dosas

One of our favorite foods to have on hand (as a batter), dosas cook in minutes and can be used as a shell for wraps, in place of bread for sandwiches (not traditionally but functionally), etc.

1 c Rice (short grain brown rice or any other that sprouts) combined with **½ c Mung Beans** or **Lentils** and sprouted 2-3 days.
Ferment Starter (1 tsp. miso or 2 T rejuvelac, water kefir, apple cider vinegar, or lemon juice combined with 1 ½ c pure water).
2 tsp. Real Salt

Blend well sprouted rice and legumes with ferment starter, pour into half gallon jar, cover with an air tight lid and let ferment at room temperature for 24-48 hrs. Stir in salt, and if necessary water to form a medium/thin batter, pour a thin layer of batter (about ½ cup) into a large non-stick skillet on medium heat, flip when batter sets and edges peel away from pan, finish cooking till well done.

Makes: **6**   Required: **B**   S/F/0% Raw

Fluffels

Less liquid but otherwise the same batter used for dosas above. Here however, instead of frying the batter is balled up and steamed to create dumpling like objects used in soups, for dipping, etc.

1 c Rice (short grain brown rice or any other that sprouts) combined with **½ c Mung Beans** or **Lentils** and sprouted 2-3 days.
Ferment Starter (1 tsp. miso or 2 T rejuvelac, water kefir, apple cider vinegar, or lemon juice combined with ½ c pure water).
2 tsp. Real Salt

Blend sprouted rice and legumes with ferment starter to form a thick batter, add more water only if necessary to blend, transfer to a half gallon jar, cover with an air tight lid and let sit to ferment at room temperature for 24-48 hrs. Stir in salt, scoop out spoonfuls of batter and roll into 1" round balls, steam balls (poacher pan works well if you have one) till firm and cooked through (15-20 min.).

Makes: **12+**   Required: **B**   S/F/0% Raw

MAIN MEALS

Fabulous 5

#2 selling sandwich at the Healthy Junk booth...but just as fabulous!

2 *Seed Crusts* (p.110) or *Veggie Seed Crusts* (p.111)
1 **Avocado** sliced.
Sauerkraut (p.145)
Red Onion julienne sliced.
Broccoli and/or **Sunflower Sprouts**
Nutritional Yeast
Dulse Flakes

Lay avocado slices on crusts, mash a bit with a fork, and layer on sauerkraut, red onion and sprouts, sprinkle on yeast and dulse flakes.

Serves: **2**   Required: **N/A**   S/F/**100**% Raw

Sunshine Sandwich

#1 best selling sandwich at the Healthy Junk booth...light, fresh, and delicious!

2 *Seed Crusts* (p.110) or *Veggie Seed Crusts* (p.111)
1 **Avocado** sliced.
¼ **Cucumber** sliced.
1 **Tomato** (preferably heirloom) sliced.
Real Salt & Pepper to taste.
Broccoli and/or **Sunflower Sprouts**
Onion julienne sliced.
Dressing of choice (optional).

Lay avocado slices on crusts, mash a bit with a fork, layer on cucumber, tomato, salt & pepper, sprouts and onion, drizzle with dressing of choice if desired.

Serves: **2**   Required: **N/A**   S/**100**% Raw

MAIN MEALS

Summer Delight

A veggie sandwich utilizing summers offerings, dosa style!

2 *Dosas* (p.113) or ***Tortillas*** (p.112)
1 c Lettuce or **Mixed Salad Greens** shredded.
1 Tomato chopped and/or **6 Sun Dried Tomatoes** soaked & diced.
¼ Cucumber diced.
¼ Red Bell Pepper diced.
¼ Red Onion diced.
Broccoli Sprouts and/or **Sunflower Sprouts**
Black Peeper & **Real Salt** to taste.
Fresh Basil chopped (optional).
Hummus (p.135) or ***Seed Cheese*** (p.132) (optional).
Salad Dressing of choice (optional).

Place all desired ingredients on dosas, fold and serve.

Serves: **2**   Required: **N/A**   S/F/60% Raw

Mediterranean Boats

Easy sailing!

1 Head Romaine Lettuce
2 c *Med Spread* (p.132)
Broccoli Sprouts
1 Tomato diced.

Scoop med spread onto lettuce leaves and top with sprouts and tomatoes.

Serves: **4-6**   Required: **N/A**   S/F/100% Raw

MAIN MEALS

Portosteak Sandwich

2 *Dosas* (p.113)
½ c Pure Water
½ Lemon juiced.
2 T Miso, Tamari, or Nama Shoyu (contains wheat).
2 Portobello Mushrooms cut into thin strips.
½ Red, Yellow, or Orange Bell Pepper sliced fine.
¼ Onion (yellow or white) sliced fine.
4 Lettuce Leaves shredded.
Cashew Cream Sauce (p.138)

In a bowl stir together water, lemon juice and miso, add mushrooms, bell pepper and onion, allow to marinade 1+ hrs., cook mixture in a skillet on medium-low heat until liquid has dissipated and veggies are soft. Place shredded lettuce onto dosas, then mushrooms, bell pepper and onion, drizzle with cashew cream sauce, eat like a Philly.

<u>Serves:</u> **2**   <u>Required:</u> **N/A**   **S/F/10%** Raw

Dhali Dolmas

Not your traditional Dhal or Dolmas, a re-incarnated version that still uses lentils and rice but in this life they are sprouted and wrapped in steamed cabbage leaves with enlightening spices.

½ c Red Lentils or other sprouted 2-3 days.
½ c Basmati or Jasmine Rice sprouted with lentils.
2 c Water
½ Lemon juiced.
1 T Apple Cider Vinegar
2 T Fresh Parsley minced.
1 T Fresh Turmeric grated fine or ½ tsp. Turmeric Powder.
½ tsp. Real Salt
½ Onion diced.
3-4 Garlic Cloves pressed or minced.
2 tsp. Mustard Seed
2 T Coconut Oil or Olive Oil
8 Green Cabbage Leaves

Cook lentils and rice together by boiling with water then simmering till tender (about 20 min.), remove from heat and drain off any excess water, stir in lemon juice and zest, apple cider vinegar, parsley, turmeric and salt, cover and let sit. Sauté onion, garlic, and mustard seed in oil till onion is soft, stir into lentil rice mixture. Prepare cabbage leaves by steaming till soft and pliable, fill with scoops of dhal and serve.

<u>Serves:</u> **2-3**   <u>Required:</u> **N/A**   **S/0%** Raw

MAIN MEALS

Shitake Stir Fry

1 c Brown Basmati or **Jasmine Rice** (preferably sprouted 2-3 days).
1¼ c Water
2 T Coconut Oil
2 c Broccolini or **Broccoli** chopped.
1 c Shitake Mushrooms sliced.
¾ c Carrots julienne sliced.
¼ c Mung Beans sprouted 2-4 days.
4 Scallions or **¼ Onion** chopped.
2 T Fresh Ginger shredded.
2-4 Garlic Cloves sliced thin.
3 T Miso (dissolved in 3 T water), **Tamari**, or **Nama Shoyu** (contains wheat).
2 T Sesame Seeds (un-hulled).

Cook rice by boiling with water then simmering till tender (about 20 min.). Toast sesame seeds by stirring in a hot skillet on medium heat till crunchy and aromatic (about 5 min.). In a wok or large skillet on med.-high heat, heat oil, add all ingredients but rice and miso, stir while cooking until veggies are tender crunchy, stir in miso, scoop mixture onto rice portions and serve.

<u>Serves</u>: **2-3**   Required: **N/A**   S/F/0% Raw

Quinoa Bowl

2½ c Water
½ c Shredded Coconut
1 c Quinoa (preferably sprouted 1-2 days).
2 c Pumpkin or other winter squash diced.
2 c Cauliflower diced.
½ Onion diced.
2-4 Garlic Cloves
1 tsp. Cumin Powder
2 tsp. Corriander Powder
2 c Dark Leafy Greens chopped.
1 T Fresh Ginger grated.
Real Salt to taste.
Cilantro or **Parsley** to garnish (optional).

Toast quinoa by stirring in a hot soup pot on medium heat till dry (about 1 min.). Blend water with coconut well, add to soup pot with quinoa and bring to a boil, add pumpkin, cauliflower, onion, garlic, coconut, cumin and coriander, cover, turn to low and simmer till quinoa and veggies are soft (about 15 min.), stir in greens, ginger and salt, remove from heat, let sit 10 min., garnish if desired.

<u>Serves</u>: **4**   Required: **B**   S/0% Raw

MAIN MEALS

Dosa Pasties

Dosas with *Mushroom Sauce* (both ferments) provide a double bonus for digestion all in tasty pasty fashion.

2 *Dosas* (p.113)
½ c *Mushroom Sauce* (p.137)
1 c Cauliflower diced.
½ c Carrot diced.
½ c Peas (fresh from pod or frozen).

While cooking dosas, use a sauce pan with water or steamer to steam cook veggies till tender soft, spread veggies onto dosas, pour on mushroom sauce, fold and serve.

Serves: **2**   Required: **N/A**   S/F/**15**% Raw

Looky Like Sushi Roll

4 Sheets Dried Nori Seaweed
Seed Cheese (p.132)
1 Avocado sliced.
Broccoli Sprouts and/or **Radish Sprouts**
¼ c Cucumber julienne sliced.
¼ c Carrot julienne sliced.
¼ c Daikon Radish julienne sliced (optional).
2-4 T Tamari or **Nama Shoyu** (contains wheat) mixed with **2-4 tsp. Wasabi Powder** (optional).
Sesame Ginger Dressing (p.97) (optional).

Holding two sheets of nori together, drag through water on a plate, allow excess water to drip off, lay sheets flat on a cutting board, fill with seed cheese, avocado, sprouts and veggies of choice, roll as tightly as possible without damaging nori, cut into bite sized pieces with a clean sharp serrated knife, drizzle on sesame ginger dressing and serve with wasabi dipping sauce if desired.

Serves: **2**   Required: **N/A**   S/F/**100**% Raw

MAIN MEALS

Squash Curry

2 c Basmati or **Jasmine Rice** (preferably sprouted 2-3 days).
4½ c Pure Water
¼ c Coconut Butter
2" Chunk Ginger peeled.
1 Lime juiced.
2 T Curry Powder
1 tsp. Real Salt or **½ tsp. Himalayan Salt**
1 T Coconut oil
3 c Winter Squash like butternut or kabocha cubed.
2 c Veggies like chopped kale, bell pepper, green beans, pea pods, onion, etc.
2-3 Garlic Cloves sliced or minced.
Cashews (optional).

Cook rice by boiling with 2½ c water then simmering till tender (about 20 min.). Blend together remaining 2 c water, coconut butter, ginger, lime juice, curry powder and salt. In a large skillet sauté squash in coconut oil till almost soft, add veggies and garlic, cook till veggies are tender but crisp, add blended ingredients, and stir until mixture is heated through, spoon over rice, top with cashews if desired.

Serves: **4**   Required: **B**   S/40+% Raw

Pumpkin Dosas

Tacos East Indian style!

4 *Dosas* (p.113)
1 T Coconut Oil
2 c Pumpkin chopped into ½" cubes.
½ Red Bell Pepper chopped.
¼ Onion chopped.
3 Garlic Cloves pressed or minced.
1 T Curry Powder
2 tsp. Garam Masala
1 tsp. Black Cumin Seed
Real Salt to taste.
Cilantro chopped.
Mushroom Sauce (p.137) or ***Cashew Cream Sauce*** (p.138) (optional).

While cooking dosas, use another skillet to cook pumpkin in coconut oil on medium heat, just as pumpkin begins to turn soft stir in bell pepper, onion, garlic and spices, cook 1-2 minutes more, spoon onto dosas, top with cilantro and sauce of choice if desired, fold or eat open face.

Serves: **4**   Required: **N/A**   S/F/5+% Raw

MAIN MEALS

Falafels

2 T Sesame Seeds (un-hulled).
1 c Garbanzo Beans sprouted 2-3 days.
2 T Flax Seed ground and mixed with **6 T Pure Water**.
½ Onion diced.
½ c Fresh Parsley or **Cilantro** or mix chopped fine.
3-4 Garlic Cloves
1 T Corriander Powder
1 tsp. each **Cumin Powder, Chili Powder,** and **Real Salt.**
¼ tsp. Pepper
Romaine Lettuce Leaves
Tahini Dressing (p.199)

Optional Toppings: diced tomato, bell pepper, scallion, cilantro, etc.

Toast sesame seeds by stirring in a hot skillet on medium heat till crunchy and aromatic (about 5 min.). In a food processor process all ingredients until well mixed and still a bit chunky, form into 2" rounds and place on oiled cookie sheet, bake at 350° for 15-20 min., flipping half way through, place on romaine leaves, top with dressing and any optional toppings.

Serves: **3-4**   Required: **FP**   S/**10%** Raw

Chickpea Lentil Burgers

½ c each **Lentils** and **Chickpeas** (preferably sprouted 2-3 days).
1 tsp. each **Cumin Powder, Chili Powder,** and **Real Salt**
½ c Cilantro chopped.
2 Garlic Cloves
1 Jalapeno or **Fresno Pepper** finely chopped.
½ Onion and **1 Red Bell Pepper** diced fine.
1 Carrot shredded.
¼ c Oat Flour
Mango Pico De Gallo (p.141)

In sauce pan cover lentils and chickpeas with water, bring to a boil, cover and simmer till soft (about 20 min.), drain, in food processor process with cilantro, garlic, pepper and spices, transfer to a bowl, stir in red bell pepper, onion and carrot, adding flour a bit at a time while working into mixture with hands, form 6 patties, fry in oiled skillet till golden brown, place on lettuce leaves if desired, top with Mango Pico de Gallo.

Serves: **6**   Required: **FP**   S/**10%** Raw

MAIN MEALS

Garbanzo Krautdog

Dogs with all the fixing's...even tails! (on sprouted garbanzos). *A dish you'll fall in love with once you get the courage to try it!*

1 Head Romaine Lettuce
1 c Garbanzo Beans sprouted 2-3 days.
2 c *Sauerkraut* (p.145)
¼ Onion (white or yellow) diced.
¼ tsp. Real Salt
½ tsp. each **Paprika** and **Garlic Powder.**
Mustard and/or *Ketchup* (p.144).

In a pan add garbanzo beans and enough water to cover, bring to a boil, turn heat to lowest setting, cover and simmer till soft, strain and let cool a bit, stir in sauerkraut, salt and spices, scoop onto lettuce leaves, top with onions, mustard and/or ketchup.

Serves: **2-4**   Required: **N/A**   S/F/**30**% Raw

Live Pizza

We hate recipes like this where ingredients are recipes, but we promised this Healthy Junk favorite would be in our book...if we ever did one! Worth the trouble if having a pizza party, you really like pizza, or want to do some food vending...not advised!

Seed Crusts (p.110) or *Veggie Seed Crusts* (p.111)
Marinara Sauce (p.136) or *Spinach Walnut Pesto Sauce* (p.136)
Mushroom Marinade (p.137)
Tomato diced.
Basil chopped.
Cashew Cream Sauce (p.138)

Spread sauce on crusts followed by marinated mushrooms, fresh tomato, then basil, drizzle on cashew cream sauce.

Serves: **?**   Required: **N/A**   S/F/**100**% Raw

MAIN MEALS

Garlic Dosa Pizza

The multi-cultured multi-functional dosa does it again!

2 *Dosas* (p.113)
1 T Fresh Sage minced or 1 tsp. dried.
1 T Fresh or **Dried Rosemary**
Marinara Sauce (p.136) or *Garlic Cream Sauce* (p.138)
Any or all of the following toppings: chopped tomato, sun dried tomato (soaked if not already soft), onion, bell pepper, olives, marinated or steamed artichoke hearts, fresh basil, fresh oregano or hot pepper flakes, *Easy Cheesy* (p.133), etc.

Prior to cooking dosas stir sage and rosemary into batter. Spread sauce onto dosas, top with toppings of choice.

Serves: **2**   Required: **N/A**   S/F/50% Raw

Vegana Lasagna

1 Zucchini (med.-large) very thinly sliced lengthwise.
½ c Walnuts *
¼ c Pine Nuts
¼ c Sun Dried Tomatoes
2 T Fresh Parsley
½ tsp. Dried Thyme
½ tsp. Dried Sage
½ Lemon juiced and skin zested.
¼ c Nutritional Yeast
½ tsp. Real Salt
Marinara Sauce (p.136)
Easy Cheesy (p.133)

With enough water to cover soak zucchini slices, sun dried tomatoes, walnuts and pine nuts together for about an hour, drain, remove and set aside zucchini, in a food processor process nuts and tomatoes with parsley, thyme, sage, lemon & zest, yeast and salt, in a baking type dish layer zucchini slices with mixture, top with marinara, sprinkle on easy cheesy, cut and serve.
Preferably soaked/sprouted & dehydrated.

Serves: **4**   Required: **FP**   **100%** Raw

MAIN MEALS

Cauliflower Alfredo

Chickpea Noodles (p.111) or **Zucchini Noodles**.
2 c Cauliflower chopped.
1 T Olive Oil
½ **Onion** chopped.
2-4 Garlic Cloves
¼ c **Pine Nuts** or **Cashews**
2 T Nutritional Yeast
½ **Lemon** juiced.
½ **tsp. Real Salt**
Pure Water as needed.
Fresh Parsley minced.
Pepper to taste.

Steam cauliflower till soft. Sauté onion and garlic in olive oil till soft. Cook noodles per recipe instructions. Blend cauliflower, onion, garlic, pine nuts, nutritional yeast, lemon juice and salt until smooth and creamy, adding water as needed to blend or achieve desired consistency. With noodles on serving plates, pour on sauce, garnish with parsley and pepper.

Serves: **2**   Required: **B**   **S/50**% Raw

Fettuzuchini No Afraido

Another favorite at the Healthy Junk booth...even though no one could pronounce it!

Mixed Salad Greens
1 Zucchini (med.-large) spiralized, turned, shredded, or otherwise made into noodles.
¾ c *Cashew Cream Sauce* (p.138) or *Cauliflower Alfredo* (see recipe above).
½ c *Mushroom Marinade* (p.137)
1 Tomato chopped (optional).

Spread salad greens onto serving plates, top with a pile of zucchini noodles, then cashew cream sauce, then mushroom marinade, garnish with tomato if desired.

Serves: **2**   Required: **N/A**   **F/95**% Raw

MAIN MEALS

Manicotti Raw

Raw and Italian aren't usually spoken together, but this dish might just have you saying "Rawma Mia"!

1 Large Zucchini sliced very thin lengthwise.
2 c *Seed Cheese* (p. 132)
2 T Fresh Parsley minced.
½ tsp. each **Dried Thyme** and **Sage.**
½ Lemon juiced and skin zested.
¼ c Nutritional Yeast
½ tsp. Real Salt
Marinara Sauce (p.136)

In a bowl stir together seed cheese, fresh and dry herbs, lemon juice and zest, yeast and salt, scoop mixture onto zucchini noodles, roll them up, cover with marinara sauce.

Serves: **4**   Required: **N/A**   S/F/**100%** Raw

Dosa Manicotti

4 *Dosas* (p.113)
2 c *Seed Cheese* (p.132)
2 T Fresh Parsley minced.
½ tsp. each **Dried Thyme** and **Sage.**
½ Lemon juiced and skin zested.
¼ c Nutritional Yeast
½ tsp. Real Salt or **¼ tsp. Himalayan Salt**
1 T Olive Oil
4-6 Garlic Cloves pressed or minced.
4-6 c Spinach chopped.
4 c *Marinara Sauce* (p.136)

In a bowl stir together seed cheese, fresh and dry herbs, lemon juice and zest, yeast and salt. In a large skillet or wok sauté garlic in olive oil for a moment, stir in spinach, cook just till wilted, place onto dosas, scoop on seed cheese mixture, roll or fold, cover with sauce.

Serves: **4**   Required: **N/A**   S/F/**80%** Raw

MAIN MEALS

Zucchini Anti-Pasta

1 Zucchini (med.-large) spiralized, turned, shredded, or otherwise made into noodles.
½ c Kale (any variety) shredded.
½ Red Bell Pepper julienne cut.
¼ c Onion (yellow or white) julienne cut.
2 T Olive Oil
½ Lemon juiced.
1 Tomato diced.
½ c Pine Nuts
8 Kalamata Olives chopped.
½ c Fresh Basil chopped.
¼ c Fresh Oregano and/or **Fresh Sage** minced (optional).
Easy Cheesy (p.133)
Real Salt & Pepper to taste.

In a bowl toss all ingredients together except easy cheesy, lay out on serving dishes and top with easy cheesy, salt and pepper to taste.

Serves: **2**   Required: **N/A**   **100**% Raw

Spicy Beans & Rice

Sprouted beans and rice give this hearty and spicy Creole dish enhanced tenderness and nutrition.

1 c Red Beans sprouted 2-3 days.
1 c Brown Rice sprouted with beans.
2 c Water
1 Bay Leaf
2 T Olive Oil
2 Celery Stalks sliced.
½ Onion chopped.
½ Red Bell Pepper chopped.
3 Garlic Cloves pressed or minced.
1 tsp. Dried Thyme
½ tsp. Dried Oregano
½ tsp. Chipotle Powder
¼ tsp. Black Pepper
½-1 tsp. Real Salt

In a sauce pan add rice, beans, water, and bay leaf and bring just to a boil, turn to low, add spices and simmer till tender. Sauté onion, pepper, garlic and celery in olive oil, stir into beans and rice.

Serves: **3-4**   Required: **N/A**   **S/0**% Raw

MAIN MEALS

Chicks & Greens

¾ c **Chickpeas** (preferably sprouted 2-3 days).
2 T Olive Oil
1 Onion (yellow or white) diced.
1 c Pure Water
3 T Tamarind Paste
3 T *Peanut Butter* (p.131 for ours or use other organic).
1 T Fresh Ginger grated.
3-4 Garlic Cloves minced.
1 T Garam Masala
1 tsp. Cumin Seed
2 tsp. Curry Powder
Real Salt to taste.
1-2 Bunches Collards, Chard, Beet Greens, or **Kale** or a mix chopped.

Cook chickpeas by boiling with enough water to cover then simmering till tender (about 20 min.). In skillet on medium heat sauté onion with 1 T olive oil for 1-2 min., add 1 c water, tamarind paste, peanut butter, ginger, garlic and spices, stir until mixture starts to bubble, stir in chickpeas, cover and remove from heat. Steam greens of choice just till wilted and tender, place on plates, top with chickpea mixture.

Serves: **2**   Required: **N/A**   S/0% Raw

Piñatas

Crisp, colorful, and muy bueno!

4 Purple Cabbage Leaves (cut in half along spine).
1 c *Bandito Dip* (p.140) or sprouted and cooked beans of choice.
½ Tomato diced.
¼ c Onion diced.
½ Avocado diced.
Spicy Gringo Sauce (p.139) or *Cashew Cream Sauce* (p.138)
Smoked Paprika or **Chipotle Powder**.

Spoon bandito dip into cabbage leaves, top with tomato, onion and avocado, drizzle with sauce, dust with smoked paprika.

Serves: **2**   Required: **N/A**   S/F/100% Raw

MAIN MEALS

Tostada

4 *Tortillas* (p.112)
Salsamole (p.140) or use chopped avocado, tomato, onion and cilantro.
1 c Red Beans or other beans (preferably sprouted 3-4 days).
1 c Water
¼ Red Bell Pepper diced.
2 Cloves Garlic pressed or minced.
1 tsp. Chili Powder
½ tsp. Dried Oregano
½ tsp. Cumin Powder
2-3 Lettuce Leaves shredded.

Bring beans just to a boil in 1 c water, turn to low and simmer till tender, stir and mash in bell pepper, garlic and spices, cover, remove from heat and let stand 10 min., spread beans on tortillas and top with salsamole, lettuce and/or other fixings.

Serves: **2**   Required: **N/A**   S/F/**30**% Raw

Enchiladas

Homemade tortillas and sauce...it doesn't get any mejor!

4 *Tortillas* (p.112)
2 c *Bandito Dip* (p.140)
½ c Black Olives sliced or chopped.
1 Tomato chopped.
4-6 c Spinach
Enchilada Sauce (p.139)
Spicy Gringo Sauce (p.139) or ***Cashew Cream Sauce*** (p.138) (optional).
Cilantro and/or **Green Onion** chopped.

Steam spinach just till wilted, place on tortillas, scoop on bandito dip, chopped tomato and olives, roll or fold, spoon on enchilada sauce, drizzle with sauce if desired, top with cilantro and/or green onion.

Serves: **4**   Required: **N/A**   S/F/**100**% Raw

MAIN MEALS

Bandito Burrito

2 *Dosas* (p.113)
1 c *Bandito Dip* (p.140)
2-4 **Lettuce Leaves** shredded.
1 **Tomato** diced.
1 **Avocado** diced.
Cilantro chopped (optional).
Squeeze of Lime Juice (optional).

Scoop bandito dip onto the center of dosas, top with remaining ingredients, fold.

Serves: **2**   Required: **N/A**   S/F/60% Raw

Sloppy Jose's

A sloppy tasty mess served on tortillas instead of buns. *Or instead of tortillas try wrapping mix in lettuce leaves.*

6 *Tortillas* (p.112)
1 c **Lentils** (preferably sprouted 2-3 days).
2 T **Olive Oil**
1 **Red Bell Pepper** diced.
1 **Onion** diced.
2-4 **Garlic Cloves** minced.
4 tsp. **Chili Powder**
2 tsp. **Mustard Powder**
1 tsp. **Smoked Paprika**
½ tsp. **Real Salt**
¼ tsp. **Black Pepper**
1 c **Sun Dried Tomatoes** soaked in **2 c Water**.
1 T **Maple Syrup**
1 T **Apple Cider Vinegar**

Cook lentils by boiling with water then simmering till tender (about 20 min.). Blend sun dried tomatoes and their soak water with maple syrup and apple cider vinegar, set aside. In a large soup pot on medium heat sauté onion, red bell pepper and garlic in olive oil for 2 min., stir in spices, cook till onions are soft, stir in sauce and lentils, simmer for a couple minutes, and scoop onto tortillas, fold and serve.

Serves: **6**   Required: **B**   S/F/0% Raw

Sauces
Spreads
Dips

SAUCES/SPREADS/DIPS

Oliveutter

Nutritional yeast imparts a savory buttery flavor along with B vitamins to make a healthy and tasty alternative to dairy butter. Use as a salad dressing base or drizzle/pour/spread on just about anything you would want butter on...because everything's better with Oliveutter on it!

½ c **Olive Oil**
¼ c **Nutritional Yeast**
½ c **Pine Nuts**
½ tsp. **Real Salt** or ¼ tsp. **Himalayan Salt** (optional).
3-4 **Garlic Cloves** pressed or minced (optional).

Blend ingredients until creamy. Store in fridge, stir before use.
For less fat and more fluff add ¼-½ cup water. More nutritional yeast can also be added if desired.

Serves: **1+ c**   Required: **B**   **60+**% Raw

Mayo

1 T **Flax Seed** ground and soaked with 3 T **Pure Water** 10+ min.
½-1½ c **Olive Oil**
½ **Lemon** juiced.
1 T **Apple Cider Vinegar**
Real Salt to taste.
1-2 tsp. **Mustard Seed** (optional).

Place flax mixture and 1 T oil in a food processor and process for 15-20 seconds, with processor running, slowly add another table spoon of oil in a steady stream, keep processing another 15-20 seconds, repeat this process a tablespoon of oil at a time until mixture is the consistency of mayo, add lemon juice, vinegar, salt and mustard if desired and process, add more oil and process if necessary.

For Wasabi Mayo: Add 1-2 tsp. wasabi or horseradish root powder.

Serves: **1+ c**   Required: **FP**   **100**% Raw

SAUCES/SPREADS/DIPS

Nut & Seed Butters

Multi purpose, nutritional and satisfying makes nut and seed butters a good food to have on hand. *Sprouting and dehydrated nuts & seeds (where designated) is highly recommended as it maximizes nutrients and minimizes anti-nutrients.*

2 c Nuts or **Seeds** like almonds*, walnuts*, pecans*, macadamia, brazil*, pine nuts, sesame*, sunflower*, or pumpkin*.

Blend in high powered blender until creamy or process through a Champion.
Tip: When using a Champion, nuts & seeds from the freezer will help keep butter and machine cooler.
For Toasted Sesame, Sunflower, or Pumpkin Seed Butter:
Lightly toast seeds in a skillet for several minutes before processing.
*Preferably soaked/sprouted & dehydrated.

Makes: **2 c**   Required: **B+** or **C**   S/**100**% Raw

Peanut Butter

Ever see peanut butter made from sprouted peanuts? Neither have we, but it made sense so here it is! *Always use organic peanuts as conventional are grown between cotton plantings which are heavily sprayed with pesticides.*

4 c Peanuts (organic, raw, shelled and preferably sprouted 2-3 days).
½-1 tsp. Real Salt (optional).

Preheat oven to 250°, place sprouted peanuts in a single layer on a shallow baking pan, bake until just under done, stirring a few times during their bake. *Bake time will be somewhere between 1-2 hrs., the tell tail sign is when peanuts are just a little chewy and start to taste like peanuts.* Remove from oven and allow to sit and cool (about 10 min.), process into peanut butter by using a high powered blender or a Champion juicer. Store in fridge.

Makes: **2-3 c**   Required: **B+** or **C**   S/**0**% Raw

Seed Cheese

A light and fluffy ferment, kind of sort of but not really like cheese, but it is smooth, creamy, and strangely addicting. Use on salads, crackers, sandwiches, etc. *We also use seed cheese in a variety of recipes making it a good food item to have on hand.*

1 c Sunflower Seeds (hulled) sprouted 1-2 days.
1 c Pure Water
½ tsp. Miso

Blend all ingredients together well. *If you have it blend in a tablespoon of previously made seed cheese to speed fermentation.* Pour mixture into a quart jar and cover with an air tight lid and let sit to ferment at room temperature for 6-24 hours. Store in refrigerator and use within 4-5 days.

Makes: **3 c**   Required: **B**   S/F/100% Raw

Med Spread

A filling or spread reminiscent of the Mediterranean...we're guessing! *Use as a spread or dip or on salad.*

2 c *Seed Cheese* (recipe above).
½ Onion diced.
½ Red Bell Pepper diced.
½ c Kalamata Olives sliced or diced.
½ c Sun Dried Tomatoes soaked 15+ min. then drained and diced.
½ Lemon juiced.
¼ c Olive Oil (optional).

In a bowl stir all ingredients together until well mixed. *Store un-used portion in fridge and use within 4-5 days.*

Makes: **4 c**   Required: **FP**   S/F/100% Raw

SAUCES/SPREADS/DIPS

Easy Cheesy

A tasty cheese *like* concoction that can be made to sprinkle or spread. *A small food processor works best for amounts shown, otherwise you may want to make a double batch if using a standard size food processor.*

½ c **Macadamia** or **Pine Nuts**
½ c **Nutritional Yeast**
Real Salt to taste.

For a sprinkable grated type cheese, process nuts and yeast together in a food processor until fine but still crumbly.
For a creamy spreadable cheese, process a little longer until smooth and creamy.

Makes: **1 c**   Required: **FP**   50% Raw

Sesame Caviar

Sounds like a stretch but first thing we both thought of after tasting this creation was "we must be rich, we're eating caviar!". A little goes a long way! *Use on crackers, in wraps, as bait, etc.*
Fact: Toasted sesame seeds are more nutritious/beneficial than raw.

2 c **Black Sesame Seeds** sprouted 2-3 days.
¼-½ tsp. **Himalayan Salt**

Spread sesame seeds onto a shallow pan or cookie sheet, sprinkle with salt, dry seeds by baking at 200° for about an hour, stirring several times during they're bake, run seeds through a Champion juicer with blank screen inserted.

Makes: **1 c**   Required: **C**   S/0% Raw

SAUCES/SPREADS/DIPS

Almond Satay

A creamy satay to serve over noodles, steamed veggies, etc.

½ c **Pure Water**
¼ c **Shredded Coconut**
2 **Dates** (if not soft soak 15+ min.).
1 T **Lime Juice**
2 **Garlic Cloves**
1 tsp. **Curry Powder**
1 T **Fresh Ginger** peeled.
Pinch of Cayene Powder
Real Salt to taste.
½ c *Almond Butter* (p.131)

Blend all ingredients except almond butter, pour into a bowl and stir in almond butter, let sit 20 minutes for flavors to meld.

Makes: **1½ c**   Required: **B**   **100**% Raw

Sauercream

A double dose of ferments combined with nutritional yeast makes this a tangy savory rich spread with loads of pro-biotic activity, vitamins, minerals and other beneficials. *Spread on crackers or crusts, use as a veggie dip, plopped on a salad, etc.*

½ c *Seed Cheese* (p.132)
½ c *Sauerkraut* (including liquid) (p.135 for ours or use other).
2 T **Nutritional Yeast**

Blend seed cheese, sauerkraut and nutritional yeast together on medium speed while adding just enough sauerkraut juice for mixture to blend smoothly.

Makes: **1½ c**   Required: **B**   **S/F/100**% Raw

SAUCES/SPREADS/DIPS

Hummus

3 c **Water**
1 c **Garbanzo Beans** (preferably sprouted 2-3 days).
½ c **Sesame Seeds** (un-hulled and preferably sprouted 2-3 days, with garbanzo beans).
¼ c **Olive Oil**
¼ c **Sun Dried Tomatoes** soaked in ½ c **Water** for 15+ min.
½ **Lemon** juiced.
1-2 **Garlic Cloves**
1½ tsp. **Coriander Powder**
1 tsp. **Cumin Powder**
½ tsp. **Real Salt** or ¼ tsp. **Himalayan Salt**
Pinch of Cayenne Pepper (optional).

Bring sprouted garbanzo beans and water to a boil, cover, turn to low and cook until tender. Toast sesame seeds by stirring in a hot skillet on medium heat till crunchy and aromatic (about 5 min.). Blend beans, seeds and all other ingredients until creamy, adding water if necessary and/or to desired consistency.

Makes: **2+ c**   Required: **B**   S/5% Raw

Sunflower Hummus

Super hummus! Provides a generous helping of protein, magnesium, iron, fiber and B vitamins. Use on salads, as a dip, spread on sandwiches, etc.

1½ c *Seed Cheese* (p.132)
1 tsp. **Apple Cider Vinegar**
½ c **Sun Dried Tomatoes** soaked for 15+ min. then drained and chopped.
½ **Onion** diced.
3-4 **Garlic Cloves** pressed or minced.
1 **Lemon** juiced.
1 tsp. **Paprika**
½ tsp. **Cumin Powder**
½ tsp. **Real Salt**
½ tsp. **Pepper**
¼ tsp. **Cayenne Pepper** (optional).

Stir all ingredients together in a bowl.

Makes: **2+c**   Required: **N/A**   S/F/100% Raw

SAUCES/SPREADS/DIPS

Marinara Sauce

Rich and bold! Use on pizza, pasta type dishes, and more.

4 Tomatoes (med-large) chopped.
½ c Sun Dried Tomatoes soaked 15+ min. in just enough water to cover.
¼ c Onion chopped.
¼ c Olive Oil
4 Garlic Cloves chopped.
¼ c Fresh Basil or 1 tsp. dried.
2 T Fresh Oregano or ½ tsp. dried.
¼ tsp. Real Salt
1 tsp. Fennel Seed (optional).
6-10 Kalamata Olives (optional).

In food processor process all ingredients to desired chunkiness.

Makes: **4 c**   Required: **FP**   **100**% Raw

Spinach Walnut Pesto

Use as a sauce on pizza or pasta dishes, a spread for crackers, a veggie dip, etc.

4 c Spinach packed.
1 Bunch Basil
¾ c Walnuts*
¼ c Olive Oil
½ tsp. each **Real Salt, Garlic Powder,** and **Onion Powder**
½ Lemon juiced.
1 T Nutritional Yeast

In food processor process all ingredients well.

Preferably soaked/sprouted & dehydrated.

Serves: **4**   Required: **FP**   **100**% Raw

SAUCES/SPREADS/DIPS

Mushroom Marinade

Use as a addition to other sauces or toppings, on pasta type dishes, pizzas, sandwiches, salads, etc.

¼ c **Miso** dissolved in ¾ c **Warm Water** or 1 c **Tamari** or **Nama Shoyu** (contains wheat).
2 T **Olive Oil**
½ **Lemon** juiced.
1 c **Mushrooms** (crimini, white, baby bella's, portabellas, etc.) sliced thin.
1 **Onion** (yellow or white) chopped.
½ c **Kalamata Olives** sliced or chopped.

In a bowl stir miso, oil, and lemon juice together, add other ingredients and stir to mix, place in fridge and allow to marinate 2+ hrs. before using. Store in fridge, use within 2 weeks. *Use marinade that is left after solids are gone, or pour off at any time, in salad dressings, etc.*

Makes: **3 c**   Required: **N/A**   F/100% Raw

Mushroom Sauce

Creamy cream of mushroom without the cream. Good on veggie noodle and other pasta type dishes, pizza, sandwiches, crackers, etc. *Used in or on several of our dishes.*

½ c *Seed Cheese* (p.132)
2 c **Shitake Mushrooms** or other.
½ **Onion** (yellow or white).
6 **Garlic Cloves** peeled.
1 T **Miso** mixed with 1 T **Water** or 2 T **Tamari** or **Nama Shoyu** (contains wheat).

Steam whole mushrooms, onion half and whole garlic cloves until onion is soft, blend with miso and seed cheese, adding more water if needed to blend and/or achieve desired consistency.
Chunky mushroom option: Pick out and set aside 4-6 mushrooms after steaming and before blending, slice mushrooms, re-introduce into sauce after it has been blended.

Makes: **1+ c**   Required: **B**   S/F/30% Raw

SAUCES/SPREADS/DIPS

Garlic Cream Sauce

½ c *Seed Cheese* (p.132)
2 c **Shitake Mushrooms** or other.
1 **Onion** (yellow or white) cut in half.
1 **Bulb of Garlic** separated and skinned but left whole.
¼+ c **Pure Water**
¼ c **Pine Nuts**
2 T **Olive Oil**
1 tsp. **Real Salt**

Steam whole mushrooms, onion halves and whole garlic cloves until onion and garlic are soft, remove from heat and let cool about 5 min., blend with seed cheese, ¼ c water, pine nuts, olive oil and salt, adding more water if needed to blend and/or achieve desired consistency.

Serves: **1+ c**   Required: **B**   S/F/30% Raw

Cashew Cream Sauce

A savory cream sauce reminiscent of cheesy Alfredo. Use as a salad dressing base, drizzle on open face sandwiches, pizzas, etc.

1 c **Cashews** soaked 4-6 hrs. then drained and rinsed.
2 T **Nutritional Yeast**
½ **Lemon** juiced.
1 T **Olive Oil**
2 **Garlic Cloves**
¼ c **Pure Water**

Blend all ingredients until smooth and creamy. *Add less or more water for desired consistency. For bolder sauce, mix in a 2" piece of fresh grated horseradish root.*

Makes: **1+ c**   Required: **B**   S/95% Raw

SAUCES/SPREADS/DIPS

Spicy Gringo Sauce

We suppose only a gringo would make a spicy Mexican sauce using cashews...oh well, just act loco and they'll leave you alone!

1 c Cashews soaked 4-6 hrs. then drained and rinsed.
1 Lime juiced.
1 Tomato chopped.
1 T Olive Oil
2 Garlic Cloves
¼ c Onion (yellow or white) chopped.
1-2 Fresh Hot Peppers or dried peppers of choice minced or ground like fresno, jalapeño, habanera, serrano, poblano, etc.
¼ tsp. Real Salt or to taste.

Blend all ingredients together, adding water if needed to blend and/or achieve desired consistency.

Makes: **2 c**   Required: **B**   S/100% Raw

Enchilada Sauce

A rich and spicy sauce to top virtually any Mexican dish. *Keep in squirt bottle and you can be as fast on the draw as Poncho Villa!*

½ c Sun Dried Tomatoes soaked in **½ c Pure Water** for 15+ min.
1 Large Tomato
2 Dates or 2 tsp. sucanat or agave.
2 tsp. Olive Oil
2 tsp. Chili Powder
½ tsp. Dried Oregeno
½ tsp. Garlic Powder
½ tsp. Cacao Powder
½ tsp. Real Salt
¼ tsp. Chipotle Powder

Blend all ingredients together (including sun dried tomato soak water) until smooth and creamy.

Serves: **3-4**   Required: **B**   100% Raw

SAUCES/SPREADS/DIPS

Bandito Dip

Seeds are the banditos that stole the beans place in this mock refried bean dip. *Nice on salads, as a dip, as filling in enchiladas, etc.*

1 Batch *Seed Cheese* (p.132)
¼ Onion (yellow or white) diced.
½ Red Bell Pepper diced.
1 Lime juiced.
1 tsp. Chili Powder
½ tsp. Cumin Powder
½ tsp. Oregano Powder
½ tsp. Real Salt

Stir all ingredients together in a bowl.

<u>Makes: **2**   Required: **N/A**   **S/F/100%** Raw</u>

Salsamole

Salsa and guacamole combine, which we seem to have invented because we've never seen it before...maybe we just need to get out more? *Serve with any Mexican style dish or use as a dip for sliced cucumbers or other veggies, chips, etc.*

1 Avocado
1 Tomato diced.
1 Fresh or **Dried Hot Pepper** of choice like fresno, habanera, red jalapeño, etc. diced fine or crushed.
½ tsp. Chili Powder
¼ tsp. Chipotle Powder (optional).
¼ c Onion (yellow/white) diced.
¼ c Cilantro chopped.
2 Garlic Cloves pressed or minced or ½ tsp. garlic powder.
½ Lime or **Lemon** juiced.
Real Salt to taste.

Place all ingredients in a bowl and mash together with a fork.

<u>Serves: **2**   Required: **N/A**   **100%** Raw</u>

SAUCES/SPREADS/DIPS

Mango Pico De Gallo

Use on Mexican dishes, burgers, salads, etc.

1 Mango (large or 2 "Ataulfo" mangos) diced.
1 Avocado diced.
½ **Red Onion** diced.
½ c **Cilantro** chopped.
½ **Lime** juiced
Real Salt to taste.

Stir all ingredients together in a bowl.

Makes: **2 c**   Required: **N/A**   **100**% Raw

Apple Butter

Raw fruit butter with option to ferment for longer storage. Use on crackers, breads, pancakes, etc. *Also try other dried fruits like apricot, pear, or fig in place of apple.*

2 c Dried Apples soaked in warm water till soft then drained.
2-4 T Maple Syrup, Agave, or **Honey**
1-2 tsp. Cinnamon
½-**1 tsp. Real Salt**
2 T Apple Cider Vinegar (optional).

In food processor process soaked fruit, 2 T maple syrup, cinnamon and ½ tsp. salt, taste and adjust as desired. Store in fridge and use within 2 weeks.

To ferment: Stir in apple cider vinegar, place mixture into a quart jar, seal with air tight lid and let ferment at room temperature for 2 days. Store in fridge, use within 2 mo.

Makes: **3 c**   Required: **FP**   **F/100**% Raw

SAUCES/SPREADS/DIPS

Dried Fruit Butter

Easy to make no sugar added fruit butter. Use crackers, as dessert topping, etc.

1-2 c Dried Fruit like figs, apricots, pears, cherries, mangos, strawberries, etc.
Pure Water

Place dried fruit in a jar and cover with just enough water to cover, seal with an air tight lid and place in a fridge for 2-5 days, blend or process to desired consistency. Keep stored in fridge and use within 2 weeks.

Makes: **1-2 c**   Required **B** or **FP**   **100**% Raw

Hot Pepper Jam

Raw and no added sugar makes these hot pepper jams pretty cool...but hot!

Habanera Apricot:
½ **c Dried Apricots** soaked 30+ min.
4-6 Dates soaked with apricots.
1 Habanera Pepper minced.
¼ **tsp. Real Salt**

Jalapeño Fig:
½ **c Dried Figs** soaked 30+ min.
1-2 Jalapeños or **Fresno Peppers** minced.
¼ **tsp. Real Salt**.

Process or blend ingredients while adding just enough soak water (from fruit soak water) to achieve a jam like consistency. Store in the fridge and use within 2 weeks.

Make these jams last longer and become even more flavorful and jam like by canning per our "Simply Good Canning Method" found in "Tips & Tidbits" chapter.

Makes: **1+**   Required: **B** or **FP**   **100**% Raw

Condiments

CONDIMENTS

Mustard

Easy great tasting mustard!

5 T Brown Mustard Seed
½ c Yellow Mustard Seed
3 T Apple Cider Vinegar
½ c Pure Water
2 tsp. Real Salt

Using a coffee grinder (or blender if you don't have one), grind brown seeds course and yellow seeds fine, combine with other ingredients and stir well, spoon into a jar, seal and refrigerate. Mustard can be used immediately but flavor will improve after 12 hours in fridge. *Keeps several months in fridge.*

Makes: **1½ c**   Required: **CG**   F/**100**% Raw

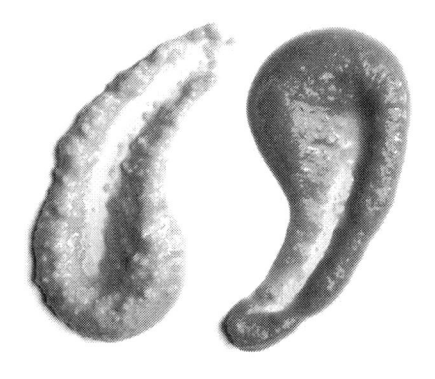

Ketchup

1 c Sun Dried Tomatoes soaked 15+ min. in **1 c Pure Water**.
½ c Raisins soaked with sun dried tomatoes.
1 Tomato chopped.
1 Pear (optional).
2 T Apple Cider Vinegar
1 t Onion Powder
1 tsp. Real Salt

Reserve tomato raisin soak water but blend all ingredients together, adding tomato raisin soak water only as needed to blend.
Tomato and pear add flavor and texture, but not required and shorten shelf life from about 1 month in fridge to less than 2 weeks.

Makes: **2 c**   Required: **B**   F/**100**% Raw

CONDIMENTS

Sauerkraut

A tangy gift for you and your tummy!

2 Heads Green Cabbage core removed and shredded (save outer leaves).
2 T Real Salt or **1 c Dulse Seaweed** soaked and sliced.

Place ¼ of sliced cabbage into a large ceramic or glass container, sprinkle with ½ T salt or ¼ c dulse, pound with a wooden mallet or pestle to release juices, repeat these steps 3 more times with remaining ingredients, cover top with outer leaves of cabbage, place as large of a plate as possible (that fits inside bowl) on top of cabbage, place a 3-5 lb. weight (large water filled jar, sterilized rock, etc.) on top of plate, cover everything with a towel or cheese cloth (to keep out pests and dirt), for the first 24 hours press down on weight/plate every few hours until juices rise above plate. *If at any time during fermentation juices are not above plate add a brine solution consisting of 1 T salt per 2 c water.* Let sit on countertop for 1-2 weeks (depending on desired taste), discard leaves, store in glass jars in fridge where it will keep for 3-4 wks.

Makes: **2+ Q**   Required: **N/A**   F/**100**% Raw

Kimchi

1 Head Napa Cabbage (small) chopped.
1 Head Bok Choy chopped.
2-3 Carrots sliced thin.
Brine (**4 T Real Salt** stirred into **4 c Pure Water**).
1 Onion (white or yellow) chopped.
3 T Fresh Ginger grated.
4 Garlic Cloves chopped.
2+ Fresh Hot Peppers chopped.
1 Daikon Radishes sliced thin (optional).
1 T Smoked Paprika or **Chili Powder**
1 T Agave or **Honey**

Combine cabbage, bok choy and carrots in a large glass or ceramic bowl and cover with brine, place a weighted plate over mixture, let sit several hours, drain and reserve brine, stir in remaining ingredients, stuff into quart jars, adding reserved brine to cover if needed, weight down contents (small dish filled with extra brine, etc.), cover jars with a cloth and let sit to ferment for 3-7 days.

Makes: **2 Q**   Required: **N/A**   F/**100**% Raw

Pickles

An easy way to get kids and picky folks to consume beneficial ferments...who doesn't like pickles!

Cucumbers (enough to fill a quart jar) soaked in cold water 10 min.
1 c Pure Water
4 T Apple Cider Vinegar
2 T Fresh Dill chopped fine.
1 T Real Salt
1 T Mustard Seed

Optional additions: Garlic cloves, bay leaf, horseradish leaf (helps pickles remain crisp).

Place whole or sliced cucumbers in a quart jar along with any optional additions, mix remaining ingredients together in a bowl, add to jar, add water if necessary to bring liquid to ½" below top of jar, cover with an air tight lid and let sit to ferment at room temperature for 3 days. *Store in fridge.*

Makes: **1 Q**   Required: **N/A**   **F/100%** Raw

Pickled Veggies

Scoop onto salads, add to sandwiches and wraps, serve as an appetizer or side dish, or consume as a most helpful snack.

3 c Vegetables like carrots, celery, hot peppers, sweet peppers, kale, onion, rutabaga, garlic, etc. chopped or sliced.
2 c Pure Water
4 T Apple Cider Vinegar, *Rejuvelac* (p.64), or *Water Kefir* (p.64).
1 T Real Salt

Place vegetables in a quart jar, combine remaining ingredients in a measuring cup or bowl with a pour spout, pour into jar with vegetables, adding more water if necessary to cover but keeping water level at least 1" below top of jar, cover with an air tight lid, let sit to ferment at room temperature for 3 days. *Store in fridge.*

Makes: **1Q**   Required: **N/A**   **F/100%** Raw

Desserts
&
Better Baked Goods

Sprout Bread

3-4 c Grains of Choice like millet, quinoa, sorghum, amaranth, wheat*, spelt*, or a mix sprouted 2-3 days.
½ tsp. Real Salt

Optional Additions: up to 1 c nuts, seeds, raisins or other dried fruit, up to 2 T spices like rosemary, garlic, cinnamon, etc.

Process grains and salt in a food processor or grain grinder, stir in any optional ingredients, shape into a loaf about ½" thick, dehydrate at 110° for about 20 hours, flipping after about 10 hours.
For baked bread shape into a loaf about ¾" thick, bake at 250° for about 2½ hours. *Bread will continue to cook after removing from oven so should be removed when crusty on the outside and still a little moist on the inside.*

*Contains gluten.

Makes: **1 Loaf**   Required: **FP**   S/**100**% Raw

Lentil Bread

Amazingly simple, nutritious, and delicious! *Excellent served with soups for dipping.*

1 c Lentils sprouted 2-3 days.
¼ c Sunflower Seeds sprouted with lentils.
¼ c Flax Seed ground.
1 tsp. Real Salt
1 T Water

Additional Options: olives, garlic, rosemary, etc.

Process all ingredients in a food processor until smooth, form into a flat loaf about ¾" thick, place on an oiled cookie sheet, and bake at 250° for 1½ - 2 hrs.

Makes: **1 Loaf**   Required: **FP**   S/**0**% Raw

Amasake

Amasake is sweet fermented rice most often used as a warm drink served with ginger, but can also be used to make puddings (see recipe below), added to smoothies, as a natural leavening and un-refined sweetening agent in baked goods, etc.

2 c Brown Rice soaked in **3½ c Pure Water** overnight.
¼ c Koji (active yeast culture) soaked in **½ c Pure Water** overnight.

Simmer soaked rice and water over lowest setting for 1 hr. or until water is absorbed and rice is very soft, let cool to about 80°, stir in koji, transfer to a ceramic or glass container, cover and let sit in a warm place for 12 hrs., stirring occasionally for uniform fermentation, place in a sealed jar and refrigerate for up to 2 weeks.

Makes: **4 c**   Required: **N/A**   S/F/**100**% Raw

Rice Pudding

Simply comforting!

2 c *Amasake* (recipe above) or **1 c Sweet Rice** (preferably sprouted 2-3 days).
½-1 c *Nut Milk* (p.67) or *Coconut Milk* (p.68)
1 tsp. Cinnamon
1 tsp. Vanilla
¼ tsp. Cardamom Powder
¼ c Raisins
¼ c Shredded Coconut (optional).

If using sweet rice, cook by bringing rice and 1¾ c water to a boil and then simmering on lowest heat till soft and sticky (about 25 min.), adding more water if needed. Remove from heat, stir almond milk into rice or warmed amasake until a pudding consistency is achieved, stir in all other desired ingredients, cover and let sit 10 minutes before serving to allow flavors to meld.

Makes: **3 c**   Required: **B**   S/F/**100**% Raw

DESSERTS & BETTER BAKED GOODS

Chia Pudding

Dessert, snack, or breakfast! *Besides healthy fats chia seeds are known for providing endurance and stamina...go get'em!*

1 c *Nut Milk* (p.67) or *Coconut Milk* (p.68)
2 T Chia Seeds

Optional additions: raisins, nuts, shredded coconut, cacao, carob, cinnamon, ripe banana (mashed in), etc. and/or sweetener of choice if additional sweetness is desired.

Stir chia with almond milk and any optional ingredients, place in fridge to set 2+ hrs., stirring after 1 hr. and/or before use.

Serves: **1-2**   Required: **N/A**   S/**100**% Raw

All-Be-Good Bars

Warning!...May all be too good!

¼ c **Coconut Oil**
½ c *Nut Butter* of choice (p.131 for ours or use other).
2 T **Agave** or **Honey**
2 T **Maple Syrup**
1 tsp. **Vanilla Powder** or 1 bean ground.
¼ tsp. **Real Salt** or pinch of **Himalayan Salt**
1 c **Oat Flakes** toasted on low heat.
½ c **Buckwheat*** (hulled).
½ c **Shredded Coconut**
¼ c **Chia Seeds**
½ c **Carob** or **Chocolate Chips** (optional).

In a small pan on lowest heat melt coconut oil, remove from heat, stir in almond butter, agave, maple syrup, vanilla and salt, stir in remaining ingredients except chips, stir in chips just till mixed, spread into a pie sized dish and refrigerate to set.

**Preferably sprouted & dehydrated.*

Makes: **12+**   Required: **N/A**   S/**75**% Raw

DESSERTS & BETTER BAKED GOODS

Yin Yang Baklava

1 c Brown Sesame Seeds (un-hulled and preferably sprouted 2-3 days).
1 c Black Sesame Seeds (un-hulled and preferably sprouted 2-3 days).
½ c Walnuts chopped.
4 T Maple Syrup or **Honey**
3 T Agave

Toast black and brown sesame seeds separately by stirring in a hot skillet on medium heat till crunchy and aromatic (about 5 min.). *To avoid popping & spattering when toasting seeds, use them as dry as possible.* Spread walnuts onto pie dish and drizzle with 1 T maple syrup, in a blender or food processor process black seeds with agave until combined, pack on top of walnut pieces, process brown seeds with remaining maple syrup, pack on top of brown seeds, cut & serve.

Serves: **16±**   Required: **B & FP**   S/**100**% Raw

Hazelnut Torte

1 c Hazelnuts*
1 c Raisins soaked 1-2 hrs. and drained.
Raw Frosting/Icing of choice (p.165).

In a food processor process hazelnuts and raisins well, mold onto a plate into a circle ¾" high, spread on frosting of choice.
*Preferably soaked/sprouted & dehydrated.

Makes: **6±**   Required: **FP**   S/**100**% Raw

Sunflower Cookies

A simple great tasting cookie to have around...never know when the cookie monster within will emerge!

2 c Sunflower Seeds (hulled) and **½ c Macadamia Nuts** soaked together 8-12 hrs. then drained and rinsed.
½ c Orange Juice
18 Dates (9 if using medjool).
1 c Shredded Coconut
¼ tsp. Real Salt
Raw Frosting/Icing of choice (p.165); *we like orange* (optional).

Process all ingredients in food processor until well mixed, roll into 1" balls, press flat to about ¼" thick onto teflex sheets, dehydrate at 110° until dry (10-12 hrs.), spread on frosting/icing if desired.

Makes: **24±**   Required: **FP & D**   S/**100**% Raw

DESSERTS & BETTER BAKED GOODS

Chocolate Chick Cookies

¾ c **Chickpeas** (garbanzo beans) sprouted 2-3 days.
½ c *Nut Butter* of choice (p.131 for ours or use other).
½ c **Sucanat** or **Coconut Sugar**
Pinch of Salt
½ c **Chocolate** or **Carob Chips** or a mix.

Process all ingredients but chocolate chips in a blender or food processor until smooth, stir in chocolate chips, drop by spoonfuls on a oiled cookie sheet, flatten, bake at 350° for 15-20 min., allow to cool before serving.

Makes: **24±**   Required: **B** or **FP**   S/**0**% Raw

Ginger Cookies

1 c **Rolled Oats**, ½ c **Buckwheat***, and ½ c **Rice*** ground to flour.
½ c **Sucanat** or **Coconut Sugar**
2 tsp. **Ginger Powder**
1 tsp. **Cinnamon**
½ tsp. **Real Salt**
1 T **Flax Seed**
3 T **Water**
3/8 c **Coconut Oil**
¼ c **Molasses**
1 T **Fresh Ginger** grated.

Blend flax and water together, let sit in blender 10 min. In a bowl mix flour, sucanat, ginger, cinnamon and salt. Add coconut oil, ginger and molasses to blender, blend with flax and water till smooth, stir into dry ingredients and into thick dough, roll into 1" balls, place 2 inches apart on a ungreased baking sheet and bake at 350° for 12 min.
*Preferably sprouted & dehydrated.

Makes: **20±**   Required: **B**   S/**0**% Raw

Right Bites

So simple it hardly qualifies as a recipe but such a quick, healthy, and deliciously balanced treat we just had to give it mention!

Dates (any variety, our favorites are "barhi", "kadrawi", and "cire").
Nut Butter of choice (p.131 for ours or use other).
Cut or tear dates just enough to remove pit, fill with almond butter.

Serves: **?**   Required: **N/A**   S/**100**% Raw

German Cacao Brownies

1 c Rolled Oats, **Oat Groats**, or **Hulless Oats**
½ **c Buckwheat*** (hulled).
1 c *Amazake* (p.149)
3 T Flax Seed
½ **c Cacao** and ¼ **c Carob Powder**
2/3 **c Coconut Sugar** or **Succanat**
2 tsp. Vanilla Powder or 2 beans ground.
¼ **tsp. Real Salt**
1/3 **c Coconut Oil**
½ **c Warm Water**

Frosting:
½ **c Shredded Coconut**
½ **c Walnuts*** or **Pecans***
½ **c Dates** soaked 15+ min.
¼ **c Coconut Butter**
3 T Maple Syrup or **Agave**.

Blend or grind oats, buckwheat and flax into flour, in a bowl stir flour with remaining ingredients (except frosting), pour into a 8x8 baking dish and bake at 300° for 30 min. Process frosting ingredients in food processor, spread on brownies while still warm.
*Preferably sprouted & dehydrated.

Serves: **9**   Required: **B & FP**   S/F/20% Raw

Beanie Brownies

1/3 **c Black Beans** sprouted 2-3 days (approx. 1½ c cooked).
2 T Flax Seed ground and mixed with **2 T Nut Milk** or water.
1-2 T Nut Milk or water (in addition to above).
½ **c Sucanat** or **Coconut Sugar**
1 T Vanilla Powder or 3 beans ground or diced fine.
½ **Avocado**
¾ **c Cacao Powder** (substitute up to ¼ c carob powder if desired).
¼ **c Walnuts** chopped (optional).
2-4 T Chocolate Chips or **Carob Chips**

Cook beans over low heat till very soft, in a food processor process cooked beans, flax, sugar, vanilla and avocado till smooth, add cacao powder and process till mixed well, adding 1-2 T of nut milk or water only if necessary to mix (batter should remain as thick as possible), stir in walnuts, spread into a 8x8 oiled baking dish, sprinkle chocolate chips on top, bake at 350° for about 25 min. (inside moist but top dry and set), allow to cool completely or chill before serving.

Serves: **12**   Required: **FP**   S/0% Raw

Rocky Roll

½ c **Dates** chopped.
¼ c **Walnuts***, **Pecans***, **Macadamia Nuts**, or other nuts chopped.
¼ c **Shredded Coconut**
½ c **Coconut Butter** & 1 tsp. **Coconut Oil** or just ½ c *Nut Butter* of choice (p.131 for ours or use other).
¼ c **Cacao Powder** or 2 T **Carob Powder** or mix of both.
¼ tsp. **Real Salt**

Place all ingredients except nuts into a bowl, mash and stir with a fork until well combined, stir in nuts, knead mixture with hands and roll into a loaf/log, slice to desired lengths.
*Preferably soaked/sprouted & dehydrated.

Makes: **2 c**   Required: **N/A**   **100**% Raw

Carob Crunch Fudge

Even if you haven't liked carob goodies in the past, this one *will* change your mind!

½ c **Coconut Oil**
1 c **Coconut Butter** or *Nut Butter* of choice (p.131 for ours or use other).
½ c **Maple Syrup** or **Agave**
2 tsp. **Vanilla Powder** or 2 beans ground.
½ tsp. **Real Salt**
1 c **Carob Powder**
2 c **Buckwheat*** (hulled).
¼ c **Cacao Powder** (optional).
½ c **Raisins** (optional).

With top 5 ingredients in a skillet and stove as low as it goes, stir continuously, just as everything begins to melt and meld together turn off heat, continue stirring while adding carob powder, buckwheat and any optional ingredients, scoop and pack mixture into a pie sized dish, refrigerate to set 1+ hrs. *Store in fridge.*
*Preferably sprouted & dehydrated.

Makes: **16±**   Required: **N/A**   **95**+% Raw

DESSERTS & BETTER BAKED GOODS

Raw Chocolate

Making your own chocolate is fun, easy, and requires *lots* of tast...testing, but best of all its however *you* like it...extra nuts, extra dark, extra spicy, some of this, some of that...

1 c Cacao Butter (cut in smaller pieces for even and faster melting).
½ c Coconut Butter
¾ c Cacao Powder
¼ c Carob Powder
½ c Coconut Sugar or **Sucanat**
1 tsp. Vanilla Powder or 2 beans ground.
¼ tsp. Real Salt

Optional Additionals: nuts, coconut, raisins, cacao nibs, chia seeds, cayenne, cinnamon, etc.

In a double boiler or pan on very low heat, melt cacao butter, remove from heat, add coconut butter and sugar, stir until coconut butter melts, stir in remaining ingredients including any additions, taste and adjust for desired sweetness, chocolateyness, etc., pour into molds or onto a cookie sheet ¼" thick, refrigerate until set (about 2 hrs.). *For quick set place in freezer for 20 min.* Break into pieces after set. *This raw chocolate is not tempered and will soften at room temperature so keep refrigerated...or get lick'n!*

Serves: ☺   Required: **N/A**   100% Raw

Raw Chocolate NOW!

For those living in the now!

2 T Cocao Powder
2 T Coconut Butter
1 T Agave Nectar
2 tsp. *Nut Butter* of choice (p.131 for ours or use other).

Stuff to cover in chocolate: dried fruit, nuts, shredded coconut, fingers, etc.)
Recipe coats about 10 cherries or macadamia nuts.

Combine ingredients in a small bowl, place in a larger bowl containing warm water, after several minutes of allowing coconut butter and nut butter to soften, stir until well mixed, coat desired food with mixture, place on a plate, freeze for 30 minutes.

Makes: **10**   Required: **N/A**   100% Raw

Rio Good Bars

Rio decadent, Rio good, Rio dangerous!

Bottom:
2 c Brazil Nuts*
2 c Shredded Coconut
14 Dates (7 if medjool; ½ c when chopped).
½ c Coconut Oil (warmed to make liquid if needed).
½ c Maple Syrup, Agave, or **Honey**

Top:
½ c Coconut Butter
½ c Cacao Powder
½ c Carob Powder
¼ c Coconut Oil (warmed to make liquid if needed).
1 tsp. Vanilla Powder or 1 bean.
1 T Maple Syrup, Agave, or **Honey**
¼ tsp. Real Salt

Process "Bottom" ingredients in a food processor until well mixed, press into a 10x10 baking dish or similar. Blend "Top" ingredients until smooth, spread evenly over "Bottom", cover and chill for 1 hour or more before serving.

Preferably soaked/sprouted.

Serves: **24±**   Required: **FP & B**   **100**% Raw

Yum Yum Yams

If you like sweet potato pie you should find this to your liking, quite decadent for being so simple, basic and wholesome.

2 Yams or **Sweet Potatoes** pealed and quartered lengthwise.
1-2 T Coconut Oil (optional).
Almond Milk (p.67)
¼ c Maple Syrup
½ c Pecans* halves or pieces.
¼ c Shredded Coconut
2 T Orange Zest (optional).

Steam yams or sweet potatoes until soft, place in serving bowls, top with coconut oil if desired, pour on almond milk, top with maple syrup, pecans, coconut, and orange zest if desired.

Preferably soaked/sprouted and dehydrated.

Serves: **2**   Required: **N/A**   **S/15**% Raw

DESSERTS & BETTER BAKED GOODS

Carrot Pineapple Aspic

2 c Rolled Oats
2 T Flax Seeds
Ferment Starter (2 T rejuvelac or lemon juice combined with 2 c pure water).
1½ c **Grated Carrots**
½ c **Dried Pineapple** diced.
½ c **Shredded Coconut**
½ c **Raisins**
1 T **Fresh Ginger** grated.
½ c **Coconut Sugar** or **Sucanat**
¼ c **Coconut Oil**
2 T **Molasses**
2 tsp. **Cinnamon**
1 tsp. **Vanilla Powder** or 1 bean.
1 tsp. **Real Salt**

Combine oats, flax and ferment starter in a large jar, cover with air tight lid and let sit at room temperature for 8-12 hrs. In a large bowl combine carrot, pineapple, coconut and ginger. Blend oat mixture with remaining ingredients (except frosting) till smooth, stir into carrot mixture well, pour into oiled 8x12 baking dish, bake at 325° for 40 min., let cool, apply frosting or other if desired.

Serves: **12±**   Required: **B**   F/**0**% Raw

Island Cakes

This recipe transforms our *Coconut Cornmeal* from "Breakfast Foods" into islands served as dessert...so if you plan ahead you can make extra for breakfast and let set in fridge as instructed below and have a pre-made dessert on hand.

Coconut Cornmeal (p.79)

After cooking coconut cornmeal as instructed, pack into small bowls and refrigerate to set 1+ hrs., tip solid corn mixture out of bowls and into larger bowls, make into islands by surrounding with almond milk, top with macadamia nuts, coconut sugar and a bit more coconut.

Serves: **2**   Required: **N/A**   F/**20**% Raw

Pie Crust

An easy delicious crust that works well for most any raw pie.

1 c Almonds * or other nut.
½ c Dates (if dates are dry then soak).
¼ c Shredded Coconut (optional...depending on type of pie).

Process all ingredients in a food processor until well mixed, press into pie dish.

If you end up with extra dough, or want to make extra, squeeze into 1" balls and roll in shredded coconut, cacao powder, carob, etc. for an awesome snack or dessert.
*Preferably soaked/sprouted & dehydrated.

Makes: **1**   Required: **FP**   **S/100**% Raw

Fruit Pie

Making good use of any seasonal fruit offerings.

1 *Pie Crust* (recipe above).
4 c Seasonal Fruit like apricots quartered, peaches sliced, soft ripe persimmons, apples sliced very thin, berries, cherries, etc.).
½ c Raisins (optional...good to use with tarter fruits like apricots or apples).
1 T Cinnamon
½ Lemon juiced.
¼ tsp. Real Salt (optional).

Place all ingredients except pie crust in a gallon size zip lock bag, seal, moosh everything around to meld flavors. *For softer fruit like apricots, peaches and soft persimmons don't squeeze so hard, for firmer fruit like apple, pears and hard persimmons squeeze a bit harder.* Pour into pie crust, refrigerate to set for 1+ hour.

Serves: **8**   Required: **N/A**   **S/100**% Raw

DESSERTS & BETTER BAKED GOODS

Choc-O-Cherry Pie

1 c Dried Cherries (no sugar added) soaked 1 hour and drained.
1 c Cashews soaked and drained with dried cherries.
1 c Fresh Cherries
1 c Young Thai Coconut Flesh
½ c Maple Syrup or **Agave**
½ c Coconut Butter
¼ c Apple Cider Vinegar
1 Lemon juice and zest.
Pie Crust (with ¼ c **Cacao Nibbs** added as option) (p.158).
Optional Topping: ½ c **Dried Cherries** and ¼ c **Cacao Powder** soaked in ¼ c **Maple Syrup** or **Agave** for 15+ min.

Blend all ingredients together except pie crust and topping, pour into crust and place in fridge till set (1-2 hrs.). For optional topping blend ingredients and drizzle on pie.

Serves: **8**   Required: **B**   S/F/85% Raw

Butternut Pie

Crust:
1 ¼ c Oat Flour (blended or ground rolled oats is fine).
¼ c Coconut Oil
¼ tsp. Real Salt
5 T Warm Water
Optional Additions: pecans, shredded coconut, cinnamon.

Filling:
2 c Butternut Squash or **Pumpkin** peeled and chopped.
½ c Cashews
½ c Sucanat or **Coconut Sugar**
2 T Chia or **Flax Seeds** ground and soaked in **6 T Water**.
1 T Fresh Ginger grated.
1 T Lemon Zest
1 ½ tsp. Cinnamon
½ tsp. Real Salt
¼ tsp. Nutmeg
¼ tsp. Clove

Steam squash till soft. While squash cooks prepare crust by using a fork to stir salt with oat flour then mashing in softened coconut oil, keep stirring while slowly adding a tablespoon of water at a time until a dough forms, press into pie pan. Blend cooked squash with all remaining ingredients, pour into crust, bake at 350° for 45-50 min.

Serves: **8**   Required: **B**   0% Raw

DESSERTS & BETTER BAKED GOODS

Cocopops

Popsicles using coconut milk as the base...after that you can go as cookoo as you want with your cocopops!

2 c *Coconut Milk* (p.68)
2 Dates

Blend coconut milk with dates, stir or blend in additional ingredients from below if desired, pour into molds (popsicle molds, Dixie or plastic cups with popsicle sticks or toothpicks, etc.), place in freezer till frozen.

Cacao Cocopops:
2 T Cacao Powder

Vanilla Bean Cocopops:
1 tsp. Vanilla Powder or 1 bean.

Karma Cocopops:
¼-½ c *Karma Sauce* (p.162)

Pina Colada Cocopops:
1 c Pineapple chopped.
¼ c Shredded Coconut

Chocolate Cherry Cocopops:
¼ c Dried Cherries diced.
¼ c Cacao Powder or **Chocolate Chips**

Strawberry Banana Cocopops:
1 Banana
¾ c Strawberries

Serves: **2-6**   Required: **B**   **100%** Raw

DESSERTS & BETTER BAKED GOODS

I Scream

A non-dairy ice cream so simple, so fast, and so guilt free it can be eaten joyfully anytime!

3 Bananas very ripe peeled and frozen.
½ c *Almond Milk* or try other ***Nut Milk*** (p.67).

Break frozen bananas into 3-4 pieces, process in a food processor or a quality blender while adding almond milk a little at a time and just till mixture becomes smooth and creamy, stopping equipment and scraping sides down as needed. *Other fresh or frozen fruits like pineapple, peach, apricot, blackberries, or cherries can be processed with bananas (bananas add the creamy texture).*

Topping ideas:
Cacao Sauce or *Karma Sauce* (p.162)
Nuts (almonds, walnuts, pecans, etc.).
Fresh Fruit
Shredded Coconut

Serves: **2**   Required: **B+ or FP**   **100**% Raw

Orange Sure-bet

A sure bet for a refreshing taste treat!

3 Bananas very ripe peeled and frozen.
2 Oranges juiced.

Break frozen bananas into 3-4 pieces, process in a food processor or a quality blender while adding orange juice a little at a time and just until the mixture becomes smooth and creamy, stopping equipment and scraping sides down as needed.

Serves: **2**   Required: **B+ or FP**   **100**% Raw

DESSERT TOPPINGS

Cacao Sauce

As good of a chocolate sauce as you'll ever lay your tongue on. Great on our "*I Scream*"...or anything else!

1 c Agave Syrup
½ c Cacao Powder or **2 T Carob Powder** or a mix of both.
1 tsp. Vanilla Powder or 1 bean.

Blend ingredients until well mixed.

Makes: **1+ c**   Required: **B**   **100**% Raw

Karma Sauce

A caramel type sauce sure to bring about some good Karma...instead of bad teeth! Use on *I Scream* or include in or on other sweets/desserts.

½ c Dates (good varieties are "barhi" or "kadrawi" which are caramel tasting, or "cire" which tastes like butterscotch).
½ c Pure Water
¼ c *Almond Butter* (p.131 for ours or use other).
1 tsp. Vanilla Powder or 1 bean.
½ tsp. Cinnamon
¼ tsp. Himalayan Salt
2 T Maple Syrup or **Agave** (optional).

Soak dates in water for at least 1 hr., blend with remaining ingredients until well blended. Store unused portion in fridge.

Makes: **1½ c**   Required: **B**   **100**% Raw

DESSERT TOPPINGS

Fruit Sauce

Simplicity at its best! *Besides desserts use on pancakes, cereals, etc.*

2 c Fresh Fruit of choice like berries, cherries, peaches, figs, apricots, persimmons, pears, etc. and/or dried fruit soaked in enough water to cover for 15+ min. (do not drain, use soak water).
¼ **c Maple Syrup, Agave,** or **Honey** (optional).
Pinch of Cinnamon, Cardamom, Cayenne, Nutmeg, etc. (optional).

Blend all desired ingredients to desired chunkiness.

Makes: **2+ c**   Required: **B**   **100**% Raw

Date Syrup

A whole raw food sweetener, use in raw dishes and deserts, for baked goods, on oatmeal or ice cream, in smoothies, etc.

½ **c Dates** torn in half and pit removed (experiment with different varieties...you can't go wrong!).
½ **c Pure Water**

Combine dates and water in a jar or bowl that allows water to completely cover dates, adding more water if necessary, cover and let sit at room temperature for 1-8 hrs., blend or mash dates in water to desired consistency. *Store unused portion in fridge.*

Makes: **1 c**   Required: **B**   **100**% Raw

DESSERT TOPPINGS

Cashew Whip

2 c Cashews soaked 2 hrs. then drained and rinsed.
3 T Coconut Oil
¼ c Coconut Sugar, Maple Syrup, or **Agave**
1½ tsp. Vanilla Powder or 1½ beans.
½+ c Pure Water

Blend all ingredients, including ½ c water, adding additional water if needed for mixture to blend smoothly, can use immediately but better if placed in a container and allowed to set up in fridge 1+ hrs.

Makes: **3 c**   Required: **B**   **100%** Raw

Coconut Cream Whip

A *cooler* whip to top your tasties!

1½ c Thai Coconut Meat
¼ c Lemon Juice
2 T Maple Syrup or **Agave**
2 T Coconut Oil

Blend all ingredients together until smooth, transfer to a jar or bowl and place in fridge to set (about 1 hr.).

Makes: **2 c**   Required: **B**   **100%** Raw

DESSERT TOPPINGS

Raw Frosting/Icing

This creamy sweet decadent frosting or icing using all raw ingredients is tops for cookies, cakes, etc.

½ c **Dates** soaked in ½ c **Pure Water** for 1+ hrs.
½ c **Coconut Butter**
2 tsp. **Vanilla Powder** or 2 beans.

For extra coconutty frosting:
After blending base ingredients, stir in shredded coconut and/or after applying frosting sprinkle on some coconut sugar.

For chocolate or carob frosting:
Blend **3 T Cacao Powder** or **1 T Carob Powder** or mix of each with base ingredients.

For orange frosting:
Soak dates in ½ c **Orange Juice** instead of water and blend with **1 T Orange Zest** with base ingredients.

For cherry chocolate chip frosting:
After blending base ingredients, add **8-10 Dried Cherries** and ¼ c **Chocolate Chips** and pulse blend once or twice.

For fresh fruit frosting:
After blending base ingredients, stir or blend in fresh fruit like sliced strawberries, raspberries, blueberries, etc.

Blend dates (including soak water) with coconut butter and vanilla until smooth and creamy.

Makes: **1½ c**   Required: **B**   **100%** Raw

INGREDIENT DEFINITIONS

Amasake - Fermented rice using **Koji** to culture. Amasake can be used as a sweetener and/or leavening agent in desserts and baked goods, eaten as a pudding, or made into a beverage. See how to make amasake in "DESSERTS & BETTER BAKED GOODS". *Most amasake found in health food stores is a pasteurized drinking product and will not work as a leavening agent.*

Agave (nectar/syrup) - A liquid sweetener produced from the agave plant, sweeter but less viscous than honey. *Agave in other than liquid form is also becoming available, but when seen as an ingredient in any of our recipes it refers to the liquid form.* Agave is a processed sugar high in fructose (as high as 90%) and implicated in such health risks as insulin resistance and increased triglyceride and uric acid levels, so like all concentrated sweeteners should be used in moderation. *Nutritionally raw honey and pure maple syrup are a better choice for a liquid sweetener!* A truly raw agave is undoubtedly a healthier option than the heated processed version most commonly available. *For truly raw agave look for a process that uses the fungus Aspergillus niger (instead of heat).*

Apple Cider Vinegar - Vinegar produced from the fermentation of apple juice. The most beneficial apple cider vinegar will be raw, unfiltered, unpasteurized and will have been produced using a "mother" culture.

Cacao - Cacao beans, nibs, and powder are the raw material from which chocolate is made. Not heated or treated with alkali and contains many more antioxidants than its refined form known as cocoa.

Coconut - For information on various coconuts and how to open them see "Coconuts" in "Tips & Tidbits" chapter.

Coconut Butter (raw) - A coconut product using raw pure unadulterated coconut meat. Smooth and creamy like a nut butter, and though sweeter can be used as such. Because of coconut butters fatty sweet taste it works well in desserts and because it's a whole food loaded with nutrients like beneficial fatty acids and minerals it's a wise choice. Not all health food stores carry coconut butter but most should be able to get it if asked, or can be found on-line (see resources). *The brand "Artisana" is widely available.*

Coconut Oil - Oil extracted from the meat of mature coconuts used by cultures for thousands of years. Found in many of our cooked recipes calling for oil because of its health benefits and ability to remain structurally stable when heated.

Coconut Sugar or **Crystals** - A granular sweetener produced from the sap of cut flower buds of the coconut palm. Tastes like a combination of brown sugar, caramel, and coconut. Less sweet than most granular sweeteners.

Dulse - A red marine algae rich in iodine and manganese. Dulse has a rich salty flavor that is less fishy than most seaweed. In flake form it makes a nice substitute for salt. In whole form it can be cut up and put on salads or in other dishes.

Ferment Starter - a substance used to begin fermentation. This book uses the vegan starters miso, rejuvelac, water kefir, apple cider vinegar, lemon and lime juice. All but lemon/lime juice contain pro-biotics to help good bacteria proliferate faster. Each imparts a slightly different flavor, so if you don't care for one try another.

Garam Masala - A northern Indian spice blend consisting of such spices as clove, cinnamon, peppercorn, cumin, and cardamom. Found in Indian or International markets and some supermarkets.

Himalayan Salt - A rock salt mined near the Himalayan mountains in Pakistan, usually pinkish or translucent to off white in color with potent salty flavor...go easy!

Kefir - A highly beneficial fermented food/beverage typically made from dairy but can also be made using water. *For more on Kefir see "Fermentation" chapter.*

Koji - Rice inoculated with the yeast culture *Aspergillus oryzae* which converts the starch in rice into a simpler sugar. Commonly fermented with rice to make **Amasake**, sake, and **Miso**.

Micro-Algae - Including **Spirulina** and **Chlorella** were some of the first life forms on the planet and the richest sources of chlorophyll of any food. Chlorophyll is both anti-fungal and anti-bacterial, detoxifies and rejuvenates, builds the blood, counteracts radiation, promotes intestinal flora, improves liver function, activates enzymes, and more! In addition to chlorophyll these algae are also high in assimilable protein, beta carotene, and the nucleic acids RNA and DNA which promote cell renewal and reverse aging. This along with algae's content of minerals, omega 3's, and the unsaturated fatty acid GLA, make them a valuable addition to most anyone's diet on a regular basis.

Miso - A fermented product, most notably from soybeans but can also be produced and obtained from non-soy foods like chickpeas (garbanzo beans). Acquire *un-pasteurized* miso to obtain the full benefits that this quality food source can provide.

Nama Shoyu - Un-pasteurized soy sauce *containing wheat*. A little milder and more delicate than the standard pasteurized variety as well as a better choice because of the beneficial qualities that living ferments provide. The brand we use and see almost exclusively is "Ohsawa", which is also organic. Not all health food stores carry Nama Shoyu, but since Ohsawa makes other soy products that many of these places do carry they may be able to get it for you.

Nutritional Yeast - Available in both powder and flake form. Used by many as a highly nutritious cheesy tasting seasoning and supplement. High in protein, iron, and many of the B vitamins including B-12. Look for yeast that is produced specifically for this purpose and classified as "primary yeast". These are of the highest quality and are typically grown on sugar beets or molasses. "Red Star" is one producer of a popular and tasty high quality yeast that we prefer and recommend. *Brewers yeast is a by-product of beer making and can contain traces of alcohol and other unwanted chemicals.*

Pure Water - Water free from chlorine, fluoride, or other chemical and toxins. *For more see "Chef Basics" in "Food Preparation" chapter.*

Real Salt - This is both a salt made by Redmond Products and a statement for the type of salt that should be used. It refers to salt that has not been heated, processed, bleached, or chemically altered in any way. *For more information on salt see "Real Salt" in "Tips & Tidbits" chapter.*

Sucanat (Rapadura) - This is minimally processed cane sugar, thus has a bit of a molasses taste. It's not raw but the best choice for a sweetener where raw is not a factor (i.e. when it will be cooked) or where an unrefined raw or liquid sugar just won't do the job. Found in most health food stores.

Tamarind - Leguminous pods of the tamarind tree, unique tastes of sweet and slightly sour. Used in drinks, entrées, desserts, etc. Whole **Tamarind Pods** include shell, strings and seeds which need to be removed before use. Purchase "select" varieties of pods with unbroken shells and preferably boxed. **Tamarind Paste** is what's left after all shells, strings and seeds are removed. Purchase pods and/or paste at well stocked grocery stores, Indian, or International Market places. **To make tamarind paste** remove shells from pods or use packaged blocks of tamarind, soak in warm-hot water (to cover) for 20-30 minutes, squeeze to break up by hand, press through a course mesh strainer to remove seeds and strings. *Store in a jar in fridge for 2 weeks or freeze (in ice cube tray).*

Umeboshi - Pickled ume fruits that impart strong tastes of sour, salty, and unique. A very beneficial fermented food to consume. Can be purchased whole as **Pickled Ume Plums** or much cheaper as **Umeboshi Paste** or **Ume Plum Paste**. A vinegar made with Umeboshi is also available.

Vanilla Powder - Ground vanilla bean, hard to find but very handy to have around (see "Mountain Rose Herbs" in "Resources").

1 tsp. vanilla powder = 1 vanilla bean.

Water Kefir - See **Kefir**.

Resources

Jaffe Bros. Inc.: (877) 975-2333
www.organicfruitsandnuts.com
28560 Lilac Road
Valley Center, CA. 92082
Mail order supplier of organic nuts, seeds, grain, legumes, and more since 1943. Quality goods and speedy shipping make these guys our choice for **broccoli seeds, oats, red beans, whole kernel corn, rice, raw peanuts, etc.**

China Ranch Date Farm: (760) 852 - 4415
www.chinaranch.com
P.O. Box 61 Shoshone, CA. 92384
Supplier of **dates**. These guys don't use pesticides or chemicals and do not steam or otherwise pasteurize their dates (which is hard to find). Besides the products on their web page they also carry economical gallon buckets of date pieces (leftover pieces from a variety of dates already pitted and chopped).

Sprout People: (887) 777-6887
www.sproutpeople.org
Organic seeds, sprouting equipment, growing instructions, recipes, etc.

Alpha Health Support: (818) 894-0066
www.ahs6.com
9018 Balboa Blvd. #120 Northridge, CA. 91325-2610
Colloidal mineral information and products.

Mountain Rose Herbs: (800) 879 - 3337
www.mountainroseherbs.com
P.O. Box 50220 Eugene, OR. 97405
Supplier of organic bulk **herbs** & **spices, teas, essential oils,** and more. Great quality control with organic and sustainable integrity.

i Herb: (951) 616 - 3600
www.iherb.com
17825 Indian Street Moreno Valley, CA. 92551
Good value and fast service for natural products like **herbs, coconut butter, super foods,** skin care, and other products.
Enter coupon code IKI615 *for first time buyer's discount!*

Rapid Raw books are other healthful recipe books by Mark & Kim, available at health food stores across the country as well as various locations on line, including our website:
www.truelivinghealthproducts.com

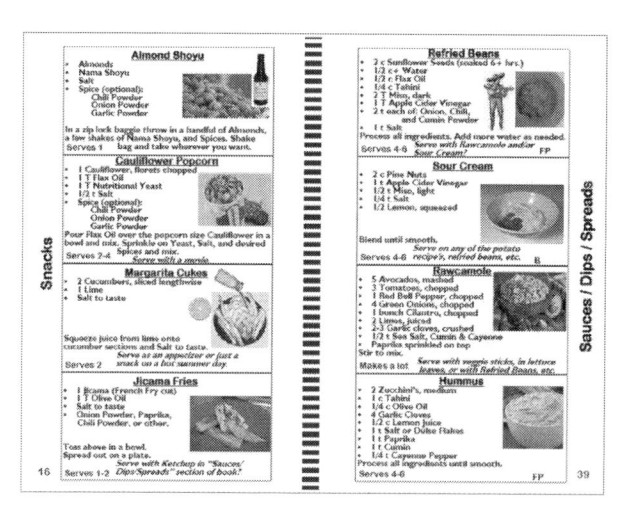

All versions of Rapid Raw books are about preparing tasty raw food dishes quickly and easily, thus allowing them to be integrated into anyone's lifestyle with satiety! It's a good book to keep handy and reference when making food choices as any recipe you choose will never let your health down nor leave your taste buds disappointed. They contain a variety of easy to prepare recipes meant to satisfy any craving at any time. Raw and living are the healthiest ways to eat most foods, but a way that is lacking in most of our diets. Rapid Raw was designed specifically as a no fuss way to add more of these beneficial foods to anyone's diet...regardless of excuse! When wise food choices like these are made *most of the time,* a high degree of health is naturally achieved and maintained.

Thank you!...

In Joy Life!

Made in the USA
Charleston, SC
13 September 2014